Royal Ceramics of
Goryeo Dynasty

NATIONAL MUSEUM
OF KOREA

Royal Ceramics of
Goryeo Dynasty

Published by the National Museum of Korea
135 Seobinggo-ro, Yongsan-gu, Seoul
www.museum.go.kr

NATIONAL MUSEUM
OF KOREA

ISBN 978-89-91331-31-0

Project Director, Lee Won-bok
Chief Editor, Kwak Dong-seok
Editor, Lee Ae-ryung and Min Byoung-chan
Assistant Editor, Kang Kyung-nam
Assistant, Song In-hee
Analysis & conservation treatments
Yu Hei-sun, Hwang Hyun-sung, Cheon Ju-yun, Jo Yeon-Tae, Jeon Hyo-soo

Authors, Kim Young-Won : Chapter I. History of Goryeo Royal Ceramics; Chapter IV. Royal Kiln
            Sites of Goryeo
          Lee Ae-ryung : Chapter II. Ceramics from Goryeo Royal Tombs (Jangneung & Gare-
            ung); Chapter III. Goryeo Royal Ceramics from Other Historic Sites (Royal Palace Site
            in Gaeseong); Chapter V. Royal Ceramics of Goryeo
          Kang Kyung-nam : Chapter II. Ceramics from Goryeo Royal Tombs (Jireung, Seongne-
            ung, Golleung, Old Tomb in Neungnae-ri); Chapter III. Goryeo Royal Ceramics from
            Other Historic Sites (Site of Hyeeumwon)

Translation, Lee Kyong-hee
Copy editing, Ted Chan
Photography, Han Jung-youp at Han Studio
Designer, Chang Dong-seok at GNA Communications
Color separation, Song Jong-seon at Graphicnet
Printing, Jungang Printing Co.

Produced and distributed by Tongcheon Publishing Co.
37-19 Haengchon-dong, Jongno-gu, Seoul
E-mail 7377419@hanmail.net
Tel. 82)2-737-7419 Fax. 82)2-737-7420

FIRST EDITION, 2009
Printed in Korea

Contents

Foreword

Ceramics is a high form of art achieved through ingenious skills in handling clay and fire. Koreans in particular attained a superb technical level of ceramic making during the Goryeo period (918-1392). Celadon vessels produced during this medieval Korean dynasty are praised for their divine beauty of form and glaze.

The primary client of the graceful celadon ware was no doubt the royal family. Some of the vessels used in the Goryeo royal household were buried in the tombs of kings and queens as funerary gifts. These royal wares provide glimpses into the highest standard of Goryeo ceramic culture. As the royal graves are clearly dated, they are also valued as definitive references in the study of Korean ceramic history as well as socio-cultural history.

This book introduces priceless ceramic objects excavated from royal graves around Gaeseong, the capital of Goryeo, which is part of today's North Korea, and Ganghwa Island, the seat of Goryeo's wartime government during the Mongol invasions in the 13th century. Also introduced are a number of high quality pieces unearthed from the royal palace site in Gaeseong; a detached palace named Hyeeumwon (House of Virtuous Grace) in Paju; and pottery shards retrieved from royal kiln sites in Gangjin and Buan.

These objects, mostly in the collection of the National Museum of Korea, exemplify the best of Goryeo ceramic ware produced by master potters. It is hoped this book will contribute to a greater understanding of the lofty standards and dignity of the Goryeo royal household and traditional Korean culture.

CHOE Kwang-shik
Director
National Museum of Korea

Legend

* This catalogue is published to introduce Korean ceramic culture abroad on the occasion of the special exhibition, "Royal Ceramics of Goryeo Dynasty," at the Fine Arts Gallery in the National Museum of Korea from December 2, 2008 to May 10, 2009.

* The catalogue describes objects displayed in the exhibition, along with some important related objects that are not included in the exhibition.

* Unless identified otherwise, most of the objects described in this catalogue are in the collection of the National Museum of Korea.

* Supplemental photos are included to enhance understanding of the exhibition's theme and are given due credit.

Celadon as Blue as the Sky

Choi Sun-u*

As rain clears and so does the fog lift,
Over the distant mountain ridge, the serene
Clear sky reveals its crisp hue.

The subtle beauty of this color
Is likened often to celadon's blue tint.
So they say it's as blue as the sky after rain.
Gazing blindly at the blue Goryeo celadon,
Truly like the distant sky after rain,
My heart feels far more tranquil.

Like old cares and wishes of Goryeo people
And their frail sorrows sifted all at once,
Never does it brag nor ridicule, but
Smiles at times and whispers now and then,
And sometimes is given to solitary thoughts.
So proud of this noble shade,
Goryeo people named it the jade color.

Reader's News (*Dokseo Sinmun*), October 7, 1971

* Mr. Choi, a distinguished art historian, served
as director of the National Museum of Korea from 1974-1984.

Map of East Asia

MONGOLIA

RUSSIA

Beijing •

• Ding kiln

KOREA

EAST
SEA

JAPAN • Tokyo

Pyongyang
Gaeseong
• Paju
Ganghwa • Seoul

Pohang
Buan • Gyeongju

Kyoto
• Osaka

Cizhou Guantai kiln •

• Yaozhou kiln
Cizhou Pencheng kiln

• Xi'an

YELLOW
SEA

Gangjin
Jin Island •
Wan Island

Hukuoka

• Ru kiln

CHINA   Nanjing •

• Shanghai

Yue kiln
• Ningbo
Jingdezhen kiln •   Guan public kiln of
the Southern Song Dynasty

EAST
CHINA
SEA

PACIFIC
OCEAN

Longquan kiln •

TAIWAN

Gaegyeong
(Gaeseong)

GORYEO

Buan kiln

Gangjin kiln

0   100   200   300   400   500   600   Miles

0   200   400   600   Kilometers

Chronologies

	Korea		China
900	918	Goryeo Dynasty founded by Wang Geon.	907	Fall of Tang Dynasty; Five Dynasties (Ten Kingdoms) begin.
	936	Goryeo achieves national unification.	916	Yao Dynasty founded by the Khitans.
	1033	Construction of wall extending 1,000 *li* to defend against more Khitan invasion	960	Northern Song begins; Song unifies Five Dynasties and Ten Kingdoms.
1100	1123	Xu Jing, a scholar diplomat of Song, visits Gaegyeong.	1115	Jin Dynasty founded by the Jurchens.
	1126	Rebellion of Yi Ja-gyeom	1124	Xu Jing of Northern Song writes *Illustrated Account of Goryeo* (*Xuanhe fengshi gaoli tujing*).
	1135	Rebellion of Myocheong	1125	Fall of the Yao Dynasty
	1170	Military officers revolt.	1127	Fall of Northern Song; Southern Song begins.
	1196	Choe family begins military rule.		
1200	1231	First Mongol invasion	1206	Mongol Empire founded; Genghis Khan declares himself ruler.
	1232	Second Mongol invasion; Goryeo moves capital to Ganghwa Island.	1219	Western expedition of Genghis Khan
	1236	Compilation of the second edition of Tripitaka Koreana (*Goryeo daejanggyeong*) begins amid wishes to solicit the assistance of the Buddha in repelling Mongol invaders.	1234	Mongols complete conquest of Jin Empire.
			1271	Kublai Khan adopts the new dynasty's name, Yuan.
	1251	Completion of the printing blocks for Tripitaka Koreana	1279	Mongols overcome Southern Song.
	1270	Return of Goryeo government to Gaegyeong		
	1281	Yuan attempts to invade Japan by mobilizing Goryeo forces.	1299	Yuan builds a Catholic church in Dadu (Great Capital), present-day Beijing.
1300	1351	Invasion of Gyeonggi coastal area by 100 ships of Japan	1351	Revolt of Red Turbans
	1356	Anti-Yuan political reform by King Gongmin	1368	Mongols are driven back to their old territory (Northern Yuan); Zhu Yuanzhang founds Ming Dynasty.
	1392	Joseon Dynasty founded by Yi Seong-gye.	1391	Northern Yuan surrenders to Ming.

Royal Tombs of the Goryeo Dynasty

	Posthumous Title	Time of Reign	Name of Tomb	Location
1st	Taejo	918-943	Hyeolleung	Gongnyeong-ri, Jungseo-myeon, Gaeseong County
2nd	Hyejong	943-945	Sulleung	Jaha-dong, Goryeo-jeong, Songdo-myeon, Gaeseong County
3rd	Jeongjong	945-949	Alleung	Alleung-dong, Yangneung-ri, Cheonggyo-myeon, Gaeseong County
4th	Gwangjong	949-975	Heolleung	Jeogyu-hyeon, Simcheon-ri, Jamnam-myeon Gaeseong County
5th	Gyeongjong	975-981	Yeongneung	Tandong-ri, Jinbong-myeon, Gaeseong County
6th	Seongjong	981-997	Gangneung	Gangneung-dong, Baeya-ri, Cheonggyo-myeon, Gaeseong County
7th	Mokjong	997-1009	Uireung	Presumably moved to the east of the city
8th	Hyeonjong	1009-1031	Seolleung	Neunghyeon-dong, Gongnyeong-ri, Jungseo-myeon, Gaeseong County
9th	Deokjong	1031-1034	Sungneung	Presumably buried on the northern suburbs
10th	Jeongjong	1034-1046	Jureung	Presumably buried on the northern suburbs
11th	Munjong	1046-1083	Gyeongneung	(Gyeongneung-ri) Jinseo-myeon, Jangdan County
12th	Sunjong	1083	Seongneung	Pungneung-dong, Pungcheon-ri, Sangdo-myeon, Gaeseong County
13th	Seonjong	1083-1094	Illeung	Presumably buried east of the city
14th	Heonjong	1094-1095	Eulleung	Presumably buried east of the city
15th	Sukjong	1095-1105	Yeongneung	Gujeong-dong, Panmun-ri, Jinseo-myeon, Jangdan County
16th	Yejong	1105-1122	Yureung	Chongneung-dong, Baeya-ri, Cheonggyo-myeon, Gaeseong County
17th	Injong	1122-1146	Jangneung	Presumably buried south of the city / Presumably buried at Byeokgot-dong, west of the city (Different records from two historical sources)
18th	Uijong	1146-1170	Huireung	Presumably moved to the east of the city

	Posthumous Title	Time of Reign	Name of Tomb	Location
19th	Myeongjong	1170-1197	Jireung	Jireung-dong, Dumae-ri, Jangdo-myeon, Jangdan County
20th	Sinjong	1197-1204	Yangneung	Yangneung-dong, Cheonggyo-myeon, Gaeseong County
21th	Huijong	1204-1211	Seongneung	Giljeong-ri, Yangdo-myeon, Ganghwa County
22th	Gangjong	1211-1213	Hureung	Location unknown
23th	Gojong	1213-1259	Hongneung	Gukhwa-ri, Ganghwa-eup, Ganghwa County
24th	Wonjong	1259-1274	Soreung	Nae-dong, Soreung-ri, Yeongnam-myeon, Gaeseong County
25th	King Chungnyeol	1274-1308	Gyeongneung	12 *li* west of Gaeseong city
26th	King Chungseon	1298, 1308-1313	Deongneung	12 *li* west of Gaeseong city
27th	King Chungsuk	1313-1330, 1332-1339	Uireung	Location unknown
28th	King Chunghye	1330-1332, 1339-1344	Yeongneung	Agyang-hyeon
29th	King Chungmok	1344-1348	Myeongneung	Myeongneung-dong, Yeoreung-ri, Jungseo-myeon, Gaeseong County
30th	King Chungjeong	1348-1351	Chongneung	Chongneung-dong, Baeya-ri, Cheonggyo-myeon, Gaeseong County
31th	King Gongmin	1351-1374	Hyeolleung	Jeongneung-dong, Yeoreung-ri, Jungseo-myeon, Gaeseong County
32th	King Wu	1374-1388		Location unknown
33th	King Chang	1388-1389		Location unknown
34th	King Gongyang	1389-1392	Goreung	Mt. Gyeondalsan, Goyang County, Gyeonggi Province

* This chronological table is based primarily on the "Report on Surveys on Goryeo Royal Tombs" from the *Survey Report on Historic Sites of the Fifth Year of Emperor Taisho*, published in 1916. Information on the tombs not mentioned in the report is from *History of Goryeo* (*Goryeo sa*) and *Augmented Survey of the Geography of Korea* (*Sinjeung dongguk yeoji seungnam*), major references compiled from the 15th to the 16th centuries under the Joseon Dynasty.

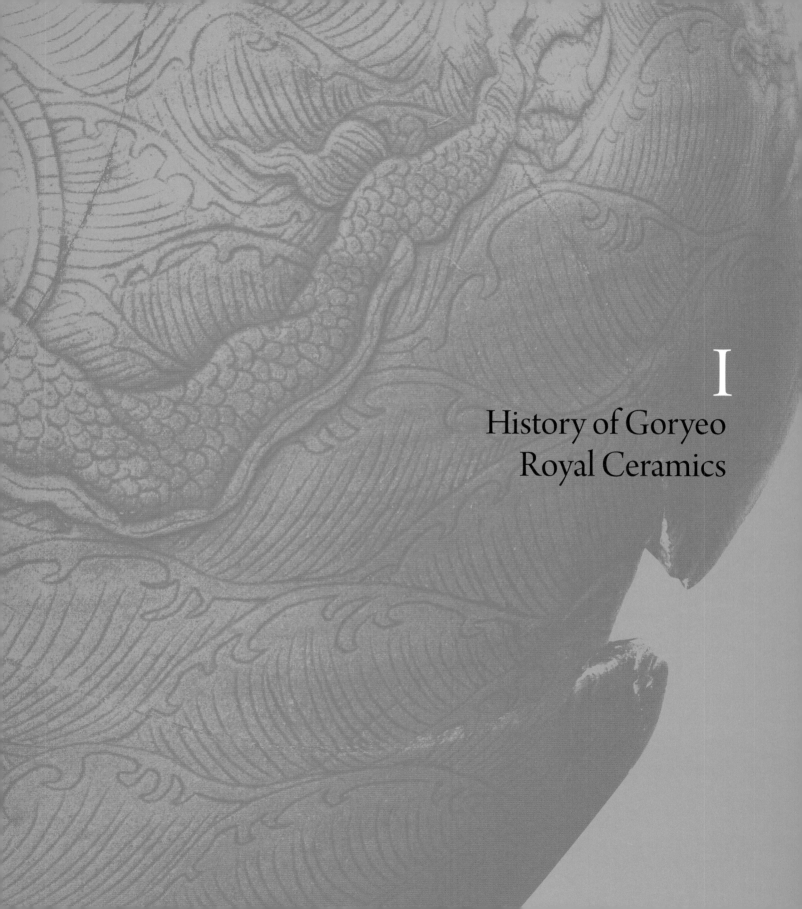

I

History of Goryeo
Royal Ceramics

I. History of Goryeo Royal Ceramics

Birth of Goryeo Celadon and Ceramic Exchange with China

Celadon began to be made in Korea in the mid-9th century during the final years of Unified Silla (676-918) and reached the peak of its development during the Goryeo period (918-1392). The style and form of early Korean celadon was influenced by Chinese imports. In the 11th century Goryeo celadon started showing its unique style. Highly prized for its jade color, Goryeo celadon vessels were shaped like humans, plants and animals and featured inlays. Although jade glaze was widely known in China, Song Chinese author Taiping Laoren praised the glaze color of Goryeo celadon as "first under heaven" in his catalogued collection of precious antiques, titled *Xiuzhongjin.*

Goryeo ware continued to be favored by the Chinese until the late Goryeo period. In the mid-Joseon period, the Korean scholar Yi Ik wrote in *The Fragmented Essays of Seongho* (*Seongho saseol*, Book IV on "Various Things") that in 1289, the 15th year of King Chungnyeol of Goryeo, Yuan China secured celadon jars and bottles from Goryeo through the Chancellery for State Affairs.

As suggested by these documents, Goryeo celadon gradually shed its early influence from Chinese wares and attained such superior quality as to be admired and imported even by the Chinese. *The Pottery Records of Jingdezhen* (*Jingdezhen taolu*), an important source on ancient Chinese ceramics published in 1815, comments on the refined style and quality of Goryeo celadon.[1] It said that the Goryeo ware had subtle glaze colors resembling those of Yue and Longquan wares, delicate patterns comparable to Ding white porcelains, and forms reminiscent of Ru ware. All these records unanimously attest to the fact that the Chinese compared Goryeo ware with the best Chinese ceramic products.

The great majority of Chinese wares imported by Goryeo are dated to Northern Song. The quantity of imports sharply decreased afterwards along with the stylistic influence from China. The quality of Goryeo celadon notably improved around the 11th century and mass production began in the 12th century. Therefore, Goryeo no longer needed to import ceramics from China.

Royal Ceramic Styles and Artifacts from Royal Tombs

Buddhism was the state religion of Goryeo and naturally had a strong impact on celadon production. The serene jade color of glazes, bodhisattvas and child monks, and lotus flowers, buds and stalks which were widely used as decorative motifs were all derived from Buddhism. Celadon objects are excavated in large amounts from ancient temple ruins. They include ritual implements and other objects marked with temple names and usages.

However, celadon wares decorated with Buddhist designs were more often used by the royal family, nobility and government officials rather than at Buddhist temples. These were usually top quality products in very refined styles. Many of these objects were inscribed with the names of royal tombs or government offices, or Chinese reign dates. Some of the superior quality celadon was used in the royal court and others were intended to be presented to aristocratic courtiers or for diplomatic exchange with China and Japan.

Study of the royal wares can be done through objects discovered at royal family grave sites, palace sites, temples and other historic places related to the royal household. Particularly, top quality royal wares have been unearthed from the tombs of several kings, including Injong (r. 1122-1146), the 17th ruler, who died in 1146; Myeongjong (r. 1170-1197), the 19th ruler, who died in 1202; and Huijong (r. 1204-1211), the 21st ruler, who died in 1237.

From Jangneung, the tomb of King Injong, various valuable artifacts were discovered, including an epitaph book, a double-layered box made up of a bronze inner box and a stone outer box, a bronze seal, a silver spoon and chopsticks, and four pieces of celadon ware (Plates 4-14). Among these, a celadon lobed vase, a celadon box and a covered cup are already widely known. These plain celadon wares have semitransparent glazes with quiet luster. They are neatly glazed down to the base, which has a few thin silica supports. Particularly, the melon-shaped vase with a foliated mouth fully demonstrates the fine aesthetics of Goryeo celadon (Plate 14).

Celadon roof tiles retrieved from the site of the royal palace of Goryeo, Manwoldae, literally the "full moon platform," suggest that high quality celadon wares were mass produced (Plate 32). Celadon roof tiles carved with gorgeous scroll designs have also been discovered from kiln sites, some with inscriptions on the back. For example, a celadon roof tile fragment found at a Sadang-ri kiln site is engraved with four Chinese characters, *nu seo myeon nam*, meaning the "southern section of the western side of pavilion." A kiln site in Yucheon-ri yielded a celadon roof tile fragment inscribed with the zodiac cycle name *gyemyo*. These are all reliable evidence of a *History of Goryeo* (*Goryeo sa*) entry in 1157, the 11th year of King Uijong, that the royal villa Yangijeong was covered with celadon roof tiles.

Goryeo celadon continued to evolve in glazing and vessel forms. Glazes became increasingly transparent, producing more crackles and making decorative patterns more elaborate. Such stylistic changes are obvious in a famous celadon bowl found in the tomb of Mun Gong-yu, an official who died in 1159, the 13th year of King Uijong (Plates 1, 93). Unearthed along with a tomb plate, the interior of this celadon bowl is densely embellished with floral scrolls in reverse inlay, which clearly show through a pure glaze. Given the quality of this vessel found in a courtier's tomb, it can be easily assumed that royal wares were even more luxurious.

Celadon objects unearthed from Jireung, the tomb of King Myeongjong, dated around 1202, are from the late 12th to the very early 13th century. Most notable among these objects is a bowl adorned with litchi scrolls (Plate 18). This bowl has a thin wall that extends from the foot to a high rim, which is slightly curved inward. The litchi scrolls, as well as other patterns, evidently look stereotypical, suggesting celadon production had already passed the peak of its development by this time. Still, bowls of this type obviously predate the mid-13th century because vessel walls grew much thicker and cruder afterwards. Therefore, this bowl is seen to represent a transitional style from the peak years of celadon making to its declining period.

Also found in Jireung, a celadon bowl with a design of clouds and cranes is in a typical early Goryeo style. The foot is high and the sides widen in the shape of an inverted horsehair hat (Plate 17). The thin vessel wall is covered with a relatively transparent glaze. The interior is decorated with an obscure relief carving of clouds and cranes.

The tomb of King Huijong, or Seongneung, dated around 1237, also yielded a number of celadon pieces (Plate 23). Though some are inferior in quality, these objects have relatively fine-colored glazes and show sophisticated styles in design and production technique.

Tombs of not only the kings but some queens also yielded celadon objects of remarkable significance. Worthy of special mention in this regard are two queen dowagers' graves: Golleung of Queen Dowager Wondeok, the wife of King Gangjong, the 22nd ruler, who died in 1239; and Gareung of Queen Dowager Sungyeong or Lady Kim, the wife of King Wonjong, the 24th ruler, and mother of King Chungnyeol, who died in 1236.

Celadon pieces found in the tomb of Queen Wondeok are decorated with various techniques, such as incising, carving and inlaying, the typical styles of the late 12th to the early 13th centuries (Plate 26). In spite of some cases where the clay is exposed due to uneven glazing, they are generally refined. The tomb of Queen Sungyeong yielded a vessel fragment similar to

1. Celadon bowl with inlaid floral scrolls

Goryeo, *circa* 1159
Excavated from the tomb of Mun Gong-yu(?-1159)
in Gaepung County, Gyeonggi Province
National Treasure No. 115
H. 6.2cm, D. 16.8cm (rim), 4.4cm (base)
National Museum of Korea

a celadon underglazed iron-painted dish found in the tomb of King Huijong, providing valuable information for comparative research (Plate 24).

The ruins of Hyeeumwon, the House of Virtuous Grace, where the Goryeo kings stayed on their tours to Namgyeong, the Southern Capital and the present-day Seoul, has been confirmed to be another treasure trove of Goryeo royal ceramics (Plates 38-48). The detached palace opened in 1122 and lasted until the early half of the 13th century. Hence the celadon objects unearthed from its site offer valuable clues to ceramic wares used in the Goryeo royal household.

Celadon works found in the tomb of Choe Hang, leader of the Choe military regime during the latter half of its control over Goryeo, who died in 1257, vividly suggest the immense power and wealth enjoyed by the military rulers. For example, a celadon gourd-shaped ewer with lotus design found in Choe Hang's tomb, which is in the collection of the Leeum Samsung Museum of Art, is far more luxurious than most royal wares from the same period (Plate 3). The ewer is an important reference for study of celadon during the latter part of the Goryeo Dynasty.

Goryeo presented gold-painted celadon vessels to the Yuan royal court in 1289 and 1297, according to *History of Goryeo* (Plates 33, 34). A broken celadon jar with a monkey design, excavated from the royal palace site in Gaeseong, shows the refined technique of applying gold paint. Another important royal ware from late years of Goryeo, a celadon bowl with scroll design is inscribed with the grave name Jeongneung. It is the tomb of Princess Noguk Daejang, the Mongolian wife of King Gongmin, who died in 1365 (Plate 2). It is believed the dish was among the vessels that were used when King Gongmin visited the tomb. The king died in 1374.

2. Celadon bowl inscribed with "Jeongneung"

Goryeo, *circa* 1365-1374
H. 7.8cm, D. 19cm (rim), 6cm (base)
National Museum of Korea

◁ **3. Celadon gourd-shaped ewer with lotus petals painted in underglaze copper**

Goryeo, 13th century
Excavated from the tomb of Choe Hang (?-1257) in Ganghwa County
National Treasure No. 133
H. 32.5cm, D. 16.8cm (rim), 11.2cm (base)
Leeum Samsung Museum of Art

II
Ceramics from
Goryeo Royal Tombs

II. Ceramics from Goryeo Royal Tombs

Jangneung: Alleged Tomb of King Injong

King Injong (r. 1122-1146), the 17th ruler of the Goryeo Dynasty, was the eldest son of King Yejong. He is known to have been benevolent and generous,[2] and well versed in music, calligraphy and painting.[3] He was invested as crown prince in 1115, the 10th year of King Yejong, and ascended the throne with support of Yi Ja-gyeom and other powerful aristocrats. In 1126 he subdued the revolt of Yi, his maternal grandfather as well as the father of his two wives, and sent him into exile. With hopes of consolidating royal authority outside of the influence of powerful noble families in the capital, he attempted to move the seat of government to Seogyeong, the Western Capital and present-day Pyongyang, as recommended by Myocheong and Jeong Ji-sang. But his plans were foiled under pressure of aristocrats in the capital. As Myocheong revolted in protest in 1135, he ordered Kim Bu-sik (1075-1151), a capital-based, pro-Chinese aristocrat, to suppress the insurrection.

Although he ascended to the throne at a young age, Injong was wise enough to set up schools in counties and prefectures around the country to promote education. Under his orders Kim Bu-sik compiled *History of the Three Kingdoms* (*Samguk sagi*) in 1145, among his various outstanding achievements. But he left problems in the aristocratic society unresolved. As a result, Goryeo under his reign is largely perceived as an era when its social order began to crumble due to irrational behavior of aristocrats. Injong died in 1146 at the age of 38. He was given the posthumous name Gonghyo, meaning "reverence and filial piety."

According to *History of Goryeo*, King Injong's tomb, named Jangneung, was placed south of the royal capital. However, *Augmented Survey of the Geography of Korea* (*Sinjeung dongguk yeoji seungnam*), compiled in the 16th century, notes that it was in Byeokgot-dong to the west of Gaeseong. In the early 20th century, the Japanese colonial government conducted a survey of historic sites across Korea. A report on the burial system of Goryeo, contained in the *Survey Report on Historic Sites of the Fifth Year of Emperor Taisho*, published in 1916, said the tomb of King Injong was in Byeokgot-dong, as recorded in the Joseon Dynasty gazetteer. But the tomb's exact location remained a mystery.

In 1916, a Japanese antique dealer sold several artifacts excavated by tomb robbers from a Goryeo royal tomb near Gaeseong, which supposedly belonged to King Injong, to the government-general.[4] These artifacts were

4. Epitaph book of King Injong and artifacts excavated from Jangneung, a tomb attributed to King Injong (r. 1122-1146)

Goryeo, first half of the 12th century
National Museum of Korea

later taken over by the National Museum of Korea after national liberation. They were King Injong's epitaph book with the inscription "Sixth Year of Huangtong," four plain celadon vessels -- a melon-shaped vase, a covered bowl, a covered cup and a vessel stand, a bronze seal, and a silver spoon and chopsticks. All of these objects are known to the public today. Also, there is a double-layered box, consisting of a bronze inner box and a stone outer box, which is displayed for public viewing for the first time.[5]

Because they were discovered and retrieved by tomb robbers, the authenticity of these artifacts has always been questioned. The celadon objects, however, show even quality with refined vessel forms and pure glazes in jade color. They all have extremely restrained decoration and the bases have silica supports. Due to these very obvious stylistic similarities, there seems to be little possibility that they were mixed up at the time of excavation. These are rather considered invaluable materials for study of Goryeo celadon as well as the Goryeo society and culture of the early 12th century.[6]

5. Epitaph book of King Injong

Goryeo, *circa* 1146
Excavated from Jangneung, a tomb attributed
to King Injong (r. 1122-1146)
L. 33cm, W. 3cm, T. 2.5cm (each tablet)
L. 33cm, W. 8.5cm, T. 2.5cm (each tablet with a
guardian god image)
National Museum of Korea

When a king or a queen died, their virtuous deeds were usually recorded in a jade book. The epitaph book of King Injong, dated "Sixth Year of Huang-tong," corresponding to 1146, is an important object providing glimpses into the political and social circumstances of Goryeo during the early 12th century. It describes Injong's character as well as Goryeo's delicate foreign relations and the positions of the king and his courtiers regarding the rebellion of the Buddhist monk Myocheong.

King Injong's epitaph book was believed to be made of jade before it was confirmed to be of calcite, a kind of calcium carbonate. It consists of 41 calcite tablets, incised with an epitaph and designed to be connected with cords, and two wider cover panels each carved with a Buddhist guardian god image. There are additional seven fragments of broken tablets that do not fit each other. The stick-like tablets have holes with a diameter of 0.6cm pierced from the sides at 4.7-4.8cm from the top and the bottom so they can be strung together with two cords. Gold powder remains on some Chinese characters (夫 and 慟) as well as the heads of guardian deities, sug-

gesting the text was originally rendered in gold script. A copper pigment is also detected on some parts of the deity images. Incised with gold script and embellished with copper red, the book originally must have looked quite gorgeous.

The composition of the epitaph book was basically influenced by Chinese jade books. For example, a jade book of Emperor Zhenzong of Northern Song Dynasty, with the inscription "The First Year of Dazhong Xiangfu," corresponding to 1008, consists of 16 jade tablets incised with gold script.[7] The stick-like tablets are strung together with two gold cords running through holes on the sides. The jade book was unearthed along with 52 jade panels decorated with dragon and phoenix designs that are believed to be components of a box. In this regard, the Buddhist deity images embellishing King Injong's epitaph book may be said to show Goryeo's unique choice of decorative motifs. The neatly incised regular script has a gentle and elegant appearance.

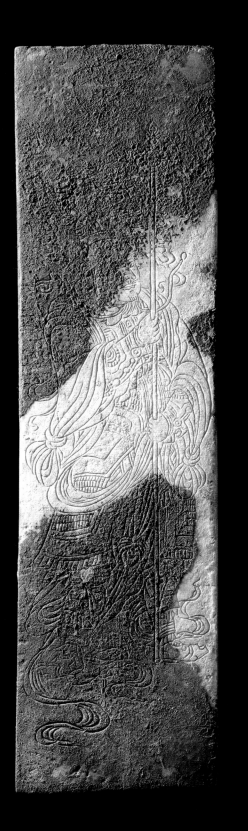

6. Guardian god images holding axes

National Museum of Korea

7. Pictorial presentations of the guardian god images from King Injong's epitaph book

The Four Heavenly Kings were popular Buddhist iconic images in China and Japan in the 10th to the 12th centuries. Of the four divine images, that is, Vaisravana (He who hears everything), Virudhaka (He who enlarges), Dhrtarastra (He who watches the land) and Virupaksa (He who sees all), two deities were usually selected to form a pair of guardians. Iconic paintings often feature two images, Vaisravana and Dhrtarastra or Vaisravana and Virudhaka at the left and right, respectively, each holding his own symbolic implement.

King Injong's epitaph book also features two of these four Buddhist deities, but both holding an axe. They were adroitly rendered with fluid lines, partly exaggerated and partly very realistic.

The Song Chinese diplomat scholar Xu Jing, who visited Goryeo in 1123, the first year of King Injong's reign, provided an interesting reference to Goryeo's iconic characteristics. Xu recorded in his book, *Illustrated Account of Goryeo* (*Xuanhe fengshi gaoli tujing*), that the Goryeo king's procession was followed by more than 10 generals of the Dragon and Tiger Royal Guards, each holding a feather fan or a gold axe. And he further noted that the gold axe resembled a pole axe.[8] As the Goryeo king was escorted during his lifetime by honor guards bearing gold axes, among other elements of ritual paraphernalia, it seems natural that his epitaph book was also decorated with guardian deity images wielding axes. The two guardian images probably symbolized the authority of the king and the royal household as well as the security of the kingdom. Similar iconic images are also found in Chinese Taoist texts. Therefore, the royal epitaph is assumed to have been influenced by the Taoist artistic tradition as well.[9]

8. Bronze seal

Goryeo, first half of the 12th century
Excavated from Jangneung, a tomb attributed
to King Injong (r. 1122-1146)
H. 7cm, D. 4.5cm (seal face)
National Museum of Korea

This bronze seal has a knob in the shape of two lions supporting a treasure bead with their front feet. The lion is regarded as a guardian of law in Buddhism. The seal face has a design composed of many curved lines, which has yet to be deciphered. Some conjecture it may not be letters but a symbolic design related with Buddhism.

Since the seal was found along with King Injong's epitaph book, it is believed to have been made to convey royal authority. The design on the seal face is also believed to have symbolized the deceased king's power. During the Joseon period (1392-1910), when a king or a queen died, a seal carved with his or her posthumous title was made along with a jade book where his or her virtuous deeds were recorded.

9. Spoon and chopsticks

Goryeo, first half of the 12th century
Excavated from Jangneung, a tomb attributed to King Injong (r. 1122-1146)
L. 32.8cm (spoon), 24.1cm (chopsticks)
National Museum of Korea

The spoon is made of silver containing a small amount of copper. It has a long-curved, thin handle with an undecorated tip. The chopsticks had been known to be made of bronze due to rust on the surface before it was confirmed to be silver. The round sticks have incised double grooves around their tips.

10. Double-layered box

Goryeo, first half of the 12th century
Excavated from Jangneung, a tomb attributed to King Injong (r. 1122-1146)
Inner box: H. 8.8cm (total), W. 31cm (the widest part); Outer box: H. 18cm (total), W. 41.8cm (the widest part)
National Museum of Korea

This double-layered box consists of an inner box shaped like a water chestnut flower and a lozenge-shaped outer box. The material of the outer box is easy-to-carve sandy mudstone, which is produced in large quantities around Pohang, a seaport in North Gyeongsang Province. It seems the box and the cover were roughly formed at first and then the carving marks were trimmed off. The surface of the cover contains slip and cinnabar, suggesting that the smoothed surface was coated with slip and then decorated with colorful pigments. The inner box has a cover and a separate stand with four legs, designed to be easily assembled. It is made of bronze and the exterior has silvery remnants from tin coating.

It is not known how this type of layered box was used, but a similar stone outer box discovered from a historic site from the Unified Silla period contained a burial urn. The box is an important object for study of the royal burial system during Goryeo.

Goryeo produced celadon cups with covers under influence from Chinese wares of the Northern Song period, mostly from the Ding, Cizhou and Ru kilns. Chinese cups produced at these kilns differed largely in the shape of knobs. Those found at the Ru kiln site of Qingliang temple have a long semi-circular knob, while the Northern Song wares from Ding and Cizhou kilns, excavated from Gaeseong and kept by the National Museum of Korea, have a flat cylindrical knob with a short coiled tail.

This covered cup found in the alleged tomb of King Injong resembles Ru ware but its knob is shaped like a lotus bud. Cover knobs found at Sadang-ri kiln sites are primarily divided into lotus bud and flat cylindrical types.

11. Celadon covered cup

Goryeo, first half of the 12th century
Excavated from Jangneung, a tomb attributed to King Injong (r. 1122-1146)
H. 9.9cm (total), D. 6cm (base)
National Museum of Korea

12. Celadon stand

Goryeo, first half of the 12th century
Excavated from Jangneung, a tomb
attributed to King Injong (r. 1122-1146)
H. 8.5cm, W. 18.3x15.2cm
National Museum of Korea

This rectangular celadon stand with a foliated top and corners is neatly formed and covered with a clean glaze without crackles. Stands in this type draw attention among Goryeo celadon wares of the 12th century, though their usage has not been identified. But its recessed top was obviously intended to hold an object and the tiered border was probably for multi-level nesting.

China continued to produce nesting vessels, which varied in form depending on their time period. They include gilt silver reliquary caskets of the ninth century Tang Dynasty, which were found in the underground crypt of Famen temple in Xi'an; a Yue celadon ware of the Five Dynasties period, dated 939; and celadon produced at the Ru kiln during the Northern Song Dynasty and the Guan public kiln of the Southern Song Dynasty. Some presume they were used to make tea.

Goryeo produced celadon stands like this under Chinese influence. Fragments of a similar stand were excavated from a kiln site at Sadang-ri, where celadon was produced during its peak years in the 12th century. The same site yielded more stands in different styles, including an undecorated round stand and a floral-shaped one carved with peonies on the sides.

13. Celadon covered box

Goryeo, first half of the 12th century
Excavated from Jangneung, a tomb attributed to King Injong (r. 1122-1146)
H. 9.6cm (total), D. 15.8cm (rim), 10.3cm (base)
National Museum of Korea

This cast celadon box is larger and taller than most other Goryeo celadon boxes of similar types. It is skillfully lobed from the shoulder of the cover down to the bottom of the vessel. The cover has two sets of double circles incised at the center and along the shoulder. A similar incised design is found around the neck of a celadon lobed vase found in the same tomb and designated as National Treasure No. 94. The box has a more refined and stable form than a Chinese cousin excavated in Gaeseong, a *qingbai* porcelain box made at Jingdezhen during the Northern Song period.

14. Celadon lobed vase

Goryeo, first half of the 12th century
Excavated from Jangneung, a tomb attributed to
King Injong (r. 1122-1146)
National Treasure No. 94
H. 22.6cm, D. 8.4cm (rim), 7.4cm (base)
National Museum of Korea

A prominent masterpiece representing Goryeo celadon of the 12th century, this elegant vase demonstrates a highly refined aesthetic sense. It has a long, gently curving neck with a foliated mouth, a melon-shaped body with fluid lines and a high pleated base, all showing an excellent sense of balance and restraint. The vase was obviously influenced by Chinese bluish white porcelain, or the *qingbai* ware, produced at Jingdezhen kilns during the latter half of the 11th century. But similar vases from Jingdezhen excavated from the Gaeseong area have shorter necks, lower bases and a generally fuller sense of volume. In China, this type of lobed vases manufactured at Cizhou, Jingdezhen and Yaozhou kilns were widely used during the Northern Song Dynasty. They were introduced to Goryeo from the late 11th to the early 12th centuries to influence local celadon production.

The Song diplomat scholar Xu Jing, who visited the Goryeo capital in 1123 and wrote about the highly prized jade color of Goryeo celadon, was probably impressed by celadon glazes of similar standard as one covering this vase. In this regard, this beautiful vase seems to have resulted from the ingenious efforts of Goryeo potters who recreated their own aesthetics, breaking away from Chinese influence. Celadon shards showing the same stylistic features as this vase were discovered from kiln sites at Sadang-ri, Daegu-myeon, Gangjin County, South Jeolla Province, which were studied by an excavation team of the National Museum of Korea in the 1970s.

15. Fragments of celadon lobed vases

Goryeo, 12th century
Excavated from kiln sites at
Sadang-ri
National Museum of Korea

Jireung: Tomb of King Myeongjong

Myeongjong, the 19th king of Goryeo who ruled from 1170 to 1197 and died in 1202, was the third son of Injong and a younger brother of Uijong. He was enthroned to replace Uijong in a military insurrection led by Jeong Jung-bu but eventually ousted by another powerful general, Choe Chungheon, and detained at Changnakgung Palace until his death.

King Myeongjong's tomb, named Jireung, is in Jireung-ri, Jangpung County in present-day Gaeseong City. It is on a small hill rising at a point where a mountain ridge stretching to the south meets with flatland. The graveyard is comfortably nestled between low mountains running in parallel directions, commanding a fine view to the south. Geomantic principles seem to have weighed heavily in selecting the site.

The Japanese colonial government started investigating this tomb after it was looted in 1916. At the time, however, the tomb already appeared to have been robbed several times and the interior of the stone burial chamber was extensively damaged. The tomb's structure was studied and burial gifts were excavated. All artifacts retrieved at the time are now housed in the National Museum of Korea.

Celadon wares account for most of the artifacts and there are some coffin nails, part of a gilt bronze ring and some Kaiyuan Tongbao coins of China. The celadon vessels include eight dishes, three bowls and a ritual vessel for emptying sacrificial wine cups. Of these, six pieces are decorated with carved or incised designs, three are undecorated, and three are inlaid.

These celadon objects, mostly for use in daily life, are remarkably simi-

16. A full view of Jireung, the tomb of King Myeongjong (r. 1170-1197, died in 1202)

Jireung-ri, Jangpung County, Gaeseong City
A glass negative of 1916
National Museum of Korea

lar to those excavated from other Goryeo royal tombs dated to the first half of the 13th century, including Seongneung of King Huijong, Gareung of Queen Dowager Sungyeong and Golleung of Queen Dowager Wondeok, as well as the site of Hyeeumwon, a detached palace. They are generally covered with clean glazes in jade color and decorated with clouds and cranes, lotus flowers and leaves, chrysanthemum, grass and flower, and litchi scrolls, all frequently found on Goryeo celadon. They are all top quality, saggar-fired wares with silica supports.

Although the tomb is clearly dated to 1202, some of the celadon objects may have been placed in the tomb when it was repaired in the wake of Mongol invasions. *History of Goryeo (Goryeo sa)* notes that the tomb was destroyed during the war and repaired in 1255, the 42nd year of King Gojong's reign.

17. Celadon objects excavated from Jireung, the tomb of King Myeongjong (r. 1170-1197, died in 1202)

Goryeo, late 12th to early 13th century
National Museum of Korea

18. Celadon bowl with inlaid litchi scrolls

Goryeo, late 12th to early 13th century
Excavated from Jireung, the tomb of King Myeongjong
(r. 1170-1197, died in 1202)
H. 8.4cm, D. 19.8cm (rim), 5.6cm (base)
National Museum of Korea

This celadon bowl is carefully decorated inside and outside. The interior has a white scroll band underneath the rim and the space below has five litchi scrolls evenly spaced apart. The exterior has a peony roundel on the central band, with the remaining space filled with an overall sgrafitto design. Inlay was done with exquisite skill but the glaze is somewhat turbid when compared with the jade color of peak years. In this regard, it may be classified with the bowls excavated from the Yongjang sanseong Fortress on Jin Island and the Beophwasa temple on Wan Island, both dated 1271 at the latest. Celadon shards in the same style have been found at kiln sites in Yucheon-ri, Buan County.

19. Celadon octagonal dish with inlaid and carved design of grass and flower

Goryeo, late 12th to early 13th century
Excavated from Jireung, the tomb of King
Myeongjong (r. 1170-1197, died in 1202)
H. 3.5cm, D. 11.8cm (rim), 6.6cm (base)
National Museum of Korea

This octagonal dish has scepter heads and lotus buds carved in low relief on the interior, while each side of the exterior has a white inlaid design of grass and flower. The low base has three silica supports neatly placed toward the inside. A similar octagonal dish was excavated from the ruins of Hyeeum-won, a detached palace, but this is far more excellent in vessel form, glaze color and inlay technique.

20. Celadon bowl with incised bamboo sprouts

Goryeo, late 12th to early 13th century
Excavated from Jireung, the tomb of King
Myeongjong (r. 1170-1197, died in 1202)
H. 5.2cm, D. 13.9cm (rim), 8cm (base)
National Museum of Korea

21. Celadon ritual wine emptier with incised lotus design

Goryeo, late 12th to early 13th century
Excavated from Jireung, the tomb of King
Myeongjong (r. 1170-1197, died in 1202)
H. 12.1cm, D. 5.8cm (base)
National Museum of Korea

Seongneung: Tomb of King Huijong

Huijong, the 21st king of Goryeo who ruled from 1204 to 1211 and died in 1237, is buried in Seongneung in Giljeong-ri, Yangdo-myeon, Ganghwa County, Gyeonggi Province. The tomb is designated Historic Site No. 369.

King Huijong ascended the throne after his father, Sinjong, abdicated in his favor. But he was dethroned by the military regime of Choe Chung-heon seven years later and suffered under military pressure until his death. Although royal power was extremely weakened and social chaos was mounting, the ousted king was buried in a graveyard carefully built to befit his royal status.

The National Research Institute of Cultural Heritage excavated the tomb in 2001. It was found to have been severely destroyed but many artifacts were found in the stone burial chamber. Celadon accounted for the most of the retrieved relics. The rest were mostly iron coffin nails and other metal objects.[10]

Celadon pieces found in the tomb are largely fragments of everyday vessels, such as cup stands and covers, jars and bottles. They are decorated with various techniques including incising, carving, inlaying and underglaze iron painting. Decorative designs include lotus petals, chrysanthemum flowers and scrolls, peony, and clouds and cranes, all widely applied on Goryeo celadon. Glazes retain the quality of jade color from its peak years, suggesting that celadon making in Goryeo maintained its high standard until the first half of the 13th century.

One of the broken celadon vessels found in this tomb has a round seal mark with a diameter of 0.8cm inside the base. Similar seal marks have been found on many celadon pieces retrieved from the Sadang-ri kilns in

22. A full view of Seongneung, the tomb of King Huijong (r. 1204-1211, died in 1237)

Giljeong-ri, Yangdo-myeon, Ganghwa County, Gyeonggi Province
A glass negative of 1923
National Museum of Korea

Gangjin, particularly No. 8, No. 23 and No. 27 kiln sites. The vessel also has beige tints that are obviously traces from gold ornament applied on the rim, as in the case of a celadon piece discovered from the site of the Hyeeumwon detached palace. Also, the vessel fragments here show the same underglaze iron painting technique as those from the Yucheon-ri kiln sites in Buan. All these findings are reliable evidence that the celadon objects buried in this tomb were top quality goods produced at the royal kilns in Gangjin and Buan.

Other important finds include coffin nails, a small amount of silver and bronze relics, beads and coins. Among these, a bronze hinge is severely corroded, with only the central section remaining, but it has traces of gold leaf applied on the surface. A bronze sheet, also decorated with gold leaf, is fixed onto a wooden element with a nail, which indicates it was part of a wooden coffin.

Given the status of the man buried in the tomb, all these relics must have been top quality products at the time. As the tomb is clearly dated, in particular, celadon pieces found here are useful references in studying Goryeo trends in ceramic production as well as characteristics of other buried objects.

23. Artifacts excavated from Seong-neung, the tomb of King Huijong (r. 1204-1211, died in 1237)

Goryeo, first half of the 13th century
Housed at the National Research Institute of Cultural Heritage

Gareung: Tomb of Queen Dowager Sungyeong

The daughter of Kim Yak-seon, Lord of Jangik from Gyeongju, Queen Dowager Sungyeong (?-1236) married King Wonjong (r. 1259-1274) in 1235, the 22nd year of King Gojong, while he was crown prince, and was invested as Crown Princess Gyeongmok.[11] She died the next year after giving birth to a son who later became King Chungnyeol (r. 1274-1308).[12] She was posthumously named Queen Dowager Sungyeong after King Chungnyeol's son, King Chungseon (r. 1308-1313), ascended the throne.

Gareung, the tomb of Queen Dowager Sungyeong, is in Neungnae-ri, Yangdo-myeon, Ganghwa County, Gyeonggi Province.[13] In 1916, the tomb was found to have been looted when the Japanese colonial government examined it.[14] But a considerable amount of artifacts was unearthed through excavations conducted by the National Research Institute of Cultural Heritage in 2004.[15]

The stone burial chamber contained 86 Chinese coins, including 19 coins of Tang and Song periods such as Yuanfeng Tongbao, which was cast from 1078-1085; a butterfly-shaped ornament; a jade ornament carved with a bird design;[16] amber ornaments and beads; a silver hinge; bronze nails and marble strips. Particularly, the white marble strips have holes on the sides in the same style as King Injong's epitaph book.[17] Although they bear no writing,[18] these marble strips were probably part of the queen dowager's epitaph book.

Ceramic objects found in this tomb include 14 celadon vessels, seven white porcelains and seven stoneware pieces. There are only two 13th century Goryeo vessels -- a celadon dish adorned with underglaze iron painted design and a celadon dish with incised decoration. Fragments of a Chinese celadon dish with carved decoration from the Yaozhou kiln of the Northern Song Dynasty were also retrieved.[19]

24. Artifacts from Gareung, the tomb of Queen Dowager Sungyeong (?-1236)

Goryeo, first half of the 13th century
Celadon fragment at far left on the back row: Present H. 1.7cm, D. 4.5cm (base)
Housed at the National Research Institute of Cultural Heritage

25. A full view of Golleung, the tomb of
Queen Dowager Wondeok (?-1239)

Giljeong-ri, Yangdo-myeon, Ganghwa County,
Gyeonggi Province
A glass negative of 1923
National Museum of Korea

Golleung: Tomb of Queen Dowager Wondeok

Queen Dowager Wondeok (?-1239) was the wife of King Gangjong, the 22nd ruler
of Goryeo. She was the daughter of Wang Seong, a royal relative and Marquis of
Sinan, but changed her surname to Yu to avoid a same-name marriage. She was
the mother of King Gojong and died in the 26th year of his reign. *History of Goryeo*
(*Goryeo sa*) highly assesses her personality.

Designated as Historic Site No. 371 in 1992, the tomb is in Giljeong-ri, Yangdo-
myeon, Ganghwa County, Gyeonggi Province. It faces the south from a gentle sloping ridge on Mt. Jingangsan. The National Research Institute of Cultural Heritage
excavated the tomb along with Gareung of Queen Dowager Sungyeong in 2004.
Eight pieces of celadon in almost perfect condition were unearthed when the gate
to the stone burial chamber was being removed. They were probably placed in front
of the gate as funerary offerings when the burial chamber was sealed.

The tomb yielded ceramics, roof tiles, various metal objects, beads and
coins. However, only two celadon dishes were found in the burial chamber, which
had already been robbed. The eight celadon vessels found on the entranceway
to the chamber included three floral-shaped dishes, an incense burner without
cover, a plum vase lid, and a bowl decorated with peony design.[20] Various decorative techniques such as incising, relief carving and inlaying coexist. But inlaid
ornaments were only found on a ewer lid and the exterior of a bowl, suggesting
a certain trend in celadon decoration at the time. Glazes on the celadon vessels
reflect the highest standard but some have greenish brown shades. All of the
vessels found in the tomb are high quality products that were fired individually
or inside a saggar, using silica supports.

Besides, the burial chamber had rings, nails and various ornaments for the coffin as well as coins. Roof tiles and a dragon-shaped ridge-end ornament and various decorative figures were excavated from the site of a ceremonial pavilion. Drawing particular attention is a silver plate attached to a piece of wood, which is believed to have been used to decorate a wooden coffin or a casket for funerary gifts. The thin silver plate, some 0.01cm thick, is fixed onto a piece of wood with bronze nails placed at even intervals. A scroll design was drawn into the plate and coated with gold. The scroll design resembles those on celadon roof tiles and pillow with a dragon design excavated from Sadang-ri kiln sites and another celadon pillow unearthed from the Hyeeumwon site, which is decorated with lotus design. Traces of lacquer coating remain on the surface of the wood.

The tomb was made in 1239, when Goryeo was struggling against Mongol invaders from its temporary capital in Ganghwa Island. The celadon objects found in the tomb indicate that the royal kilns at Gangjin and Buan continued to ship their high quality products to Ganghwa.

26. Artifacts from Golleung, the tomb of Queen Dowager Wondeok (?-1239)

Goryeo, first half of the 13th century
Incense burner at the far right in the back row: H. 8cm, D. 14.7cm (the widest part)
Housed at the National Research Institute of Cultural Heritage

Old Tomb in Neungnae-ri

This old tomb is in Neungnae-ri, Yangdo-myeon, Ganghwa County, some 70m away from Gareung, the tomb of Queen Dowager Sungyeong.

Although its name has been forgotten, the tomb was confirmed to be a royal burial site through excavation. In a surface investigation in 2004, which was conducted when the two nearby royal tombs, Gareung and Golleung, were excavated, it was found to be abandoned amid thickets of scrub trees, with the entrance to the burial chamber left partly exposed by looters. Then, in 2006 the National Research Institute of Cultural Heritage conducted a full-fledged excavation.

At the time, more than two-thirds of the space inside the stone burial chamber was found to be filled with dirt. Several wood pieces, some coated with lacquer, were unearthed when the dirt was removed. The wood pieces are assumed to have been parts of a coffin or a burial gift box. X-rays revealed traces of nailing and more than three coats of lacquer. Few artifacts escaped tomb robbers, except for several celadon shards, metal ornaments and iron nails.[21]

Celadon pieces retrieved from this tomb included fragments of bowls, dishes and an incense burner that are decorated with varied methods such as incising, carving and inlaying. Most of the pieces have glazes reminiscent of the jade color of peak years, similar to those found in Seongneung, Gareung and Golleung. Celadon pieces believed to have been made after the 14th century were also retrieved outside the burial chamber. They include a

27. The old tomb in Neungnae-ri after excavation

Excavated by the National Research Institute of Cultural Heritage in 2006 cylindrical incense burner, of which only part of the body and rim remain. The body has an embossed design of a rolling dragon and waves, and the rim has a fret design. Although the decoration is unclear and the glaze slightly oxidized, the dragon suggests the unusual status of the buried person.

Among the artifacts found inside the burial chamber are two notable silver objects, a gilt silver ornament with a phoenix design and a small gilt silver box. The gilt silver plate, broken into many pieces, is as thin as 0.5 millimeters but the embossed phoenix suggests that a queen was buried in the tomb. The phoenix has shrewd eyes and nose, and these parts are coated with gold.

The gilt silver small box was also found in broken fragments. It is made of silver plates, some 0.6 millimeters thick and divided into different sections, each embossed with grass flowers and coated with gold. The base, the top side of cover, and parts of the body are all that remain.

These survey results raised the possibility that a queen was buried in the tomb. Queen Seongpyeong (?-1247), the wife of King Huijong, or Queen Dowager Anhye (?-1232), the wife of King Gojong, whose burial sites are not known, might have been buried here. Further research on historical documents and other verification procedures is needed before reaching a conclusion.

28. Artifacts from the old tomb in Neungnae-ri

Goryeo, first half of the 13th century
Far right on the front row: Present L. 6.4cm
Left on the back row: H. 9.6cm
Housed at the National Research Institute of Cultural Heritage

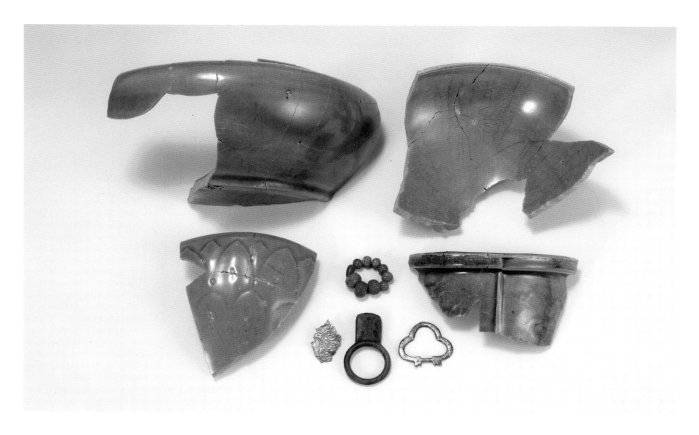

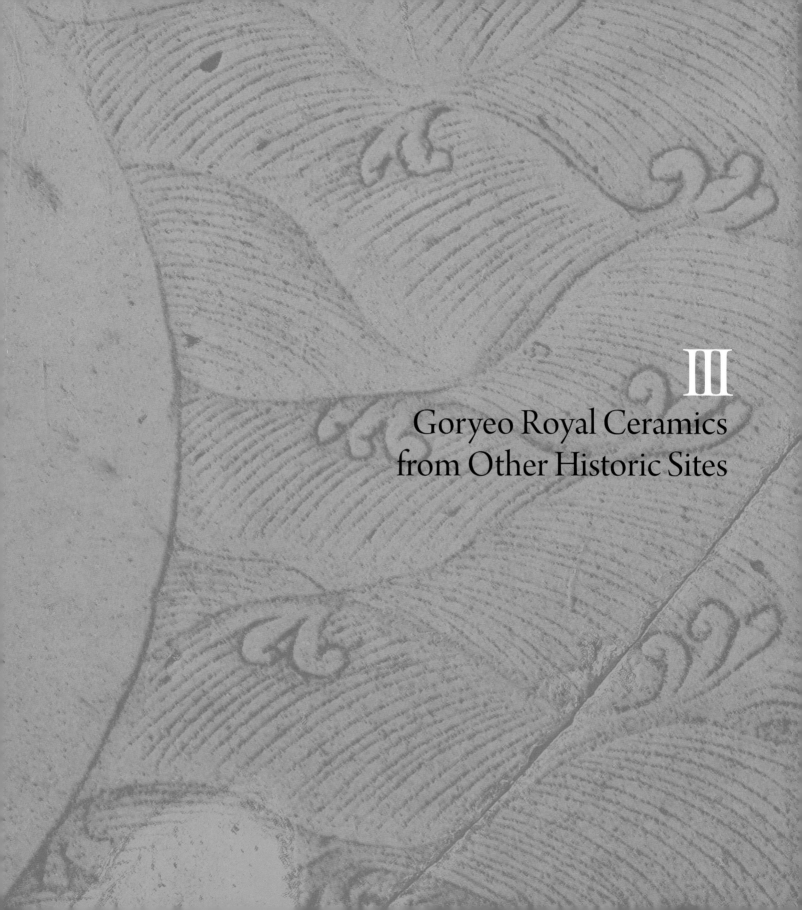

III

Goryeo Royal Ceramics
from Other Historic Sites

III. Goryeo Royal Ceramics from Other Historic Sites

Royal Palace Site in Gaeseong

Manwoldae, or the "Full Moon Platform," on the southern foot of Mt. Songaksan in Gaeseong City, is the site of the royal palace of the Goryeo Dynasty. From 919, the second year of the founding monarch, Taejo, it served as the main place of Goryeo for four and a half centuries before it was burnt down by Red Turbans in 1361, the 10th year of King Gongmin (r. 1351-1374). It was called the "main palace" (*bongwol*) during Goryeo,[22] and the name "Manwoldae" was given to its ruins during the subsequent Joseon period. Manwoldae was originally the name of the staircases leading to the main throne hall, according to *Augmented Survey of the Geography of Korea* (*Sinjeung dongguk yeoji seungnam*), compiled in the 16th century.[23]

29. A general view of the royal palace site in Gaeseong

A glass negative of 1918
National Museum of Korea

30. Site of Hoegyeongjeon, the main throne hall

A glass negative of 1918
National Museum of Korea

The Song diplomat scholar Xu Jing, who visited Gaegyeong, the present-day Gaeseong, in 1123, the first year of King Injong's reign, recorded his impressions of the palace in his book, *Illustrated Account of Goryeo* (*Xuanhe fengshi gaoli tujing*). Xu wrote that the Goryeo palace did not adhere to Chinese rules on palace composition but was designed to enliven its natural surroundings. According to Xu, the palace looked majestic and mysterious when it was seen from afar, as its many buildings, including the main throne hall, Hoegyeongjeon (Hall of Meeting Felicitation), stood on different levels connected with staircases along a sloping terrain.[24]

Despite its historical significance, the palace site was abandoned for a long time[25] before North Korean scholars mounted the first survey and excavation of the locale in 1973-74.[26] Then, in 2007-2008, the South Korean National Research Institute of Cultural Heritage and the Inter-Korean Council of Historians jointly excavated the site to nominate it for the UNESCO World Heritage List.

Some 100 roof tiles with inscriptions were retrieved along with celadon and stoneware pieces during an excavation in 2007. The roof tile inscriptions, *"jeokhang munchang"* (赤項文昌), *"jeokhang gyeongbu"* (赤項京夫), *"jeokhang hyemun"* (赤項惠文) and *"jeokhang mungyeong"* (赤項文京), have never been seen on any ancient relics excavated in South Korea. Particularly noteworthy are the inscriptions, *"panjeok sugeum"* (板積水金) and *"wolgae"* (月盖), which are obviously related with the roof tile factories named "Panjeogyo"[27] and "Wolgaeyo,"[28] both mentioned in *History of Goryeo* (*Goryeo sa*). A cylindrical celadon vessel also draws attention as an interesting object for ceramic studies.[29] How this 60cm-long vessel was used has yet to be determined.

31. Celadon fragments excavated from the royal palace site in Gaeseong

Collected before 1945
Left on the back row: H. 2.3cm
Right on the back row: H. 6.8cm, D. 4cm (rim)
National Museum of Korea

32. Celadon roof tiles

Goryeo, 12th century
Excavated from a kiln site at Sadang-ri
L. 40.8cm (total), W. 20.3cm (concave), D. 8-8.4cm (convex)
National Museum of Korea

It was first learned in 1927 that celadon roof tiles were used in Goryeo,[30] and in 1964-65, large amounts of them were excavated from the No. 7 kiln site in Sadang-ri, Daegu-myeon, Gangjin County, by the National Museum of Korea. These finds supported the record in *History of Goryeo* (*Goryeo sa*) that "Yangijeong was erected in the palace garden in the 11th year of King Uijong (the year corresponds to 1157) and the pavilion was covered with celadon roof tiles." The celadon roof tiles found at Sadang-ri were in various types, including concave tiles, convex tiles, roof-end tiles and special tiles. Some had inscriptions on the back, such as "*nu seo myeon nam*" (樓西面南, southern section of the western side of pavilion), "*seoru*" (西樓, western pavilion), "*nam*" (南, south) and "*i*" (二, two). These inscriptions suggest that celadon roof tiles were produced in accordance to specific plans.[31] Various decorative techniques such as incising, carving and relief carving were employed, while there are some plain tiles as well. Inlay was not applied on roof tiles.

33. Celadon flattened jar with inlaid monkey and gold ornament

Goryeo, second half of the 13th century
Excavated from the royal palace site in Gaeseong
Present H. 25.5cm, D. 9.3cm (base); National Museum of Korea

According to *History of Goryeo* (*Goryeo sa*), the Goryeo court presented gold-coated crude stoneware to Yuan in the 23rd year of King Chungnyeol (corresponding to 1297) and the Goryeo envoy Jo In-gyu offered gold-painted porcelain ware as a tribute to Yuan Emperor Shizu (r. 1271-1294). It is not known when Jo offered the tribute but the same source notes that he visited Yuan more than 30 times from 1275, the first year of King Chungnyeol's reign, to 1308, when the king died.[32] Therefore, it can be assumed that Goryeo produced gold-painted porcelains as tributes to Yuan during the latter half of the 13th century.

This flattened jar was found in 1933 on the ginseng drying field to the east of the Goryeo royal palace site in Gaeseong.[33] With overglaze gold ornament, the celadon jar is estimated as an important object supporting the abovementioned record in *History of Goryeo*. It has an inlaid design of a monkey holding a peach under a tree in a floral-shaped panel, which is surrounded by *baoxianghua* scrolls. Traces of gold painting remain here and there along the outlines of inlaid decoration.

The gold ornament on Goryeo celadon had long been assumed to be gold wire inlaid by scratching the glaze surface with a carving knife,[34] or brush painting done with a mixture of gold powder and adhesive substance.[35] But a recent analysis by the conservation science team of the National Museum of Korea confirmed that the gold ornament was applied with a brush along the outlines of inlaid designs and then the jar was fired again in low flames of some 700-800 degrees Celsius. The scratches on the surface of the jar, which had previously been believed to be traces of gold wire inlay, were found to be crackles that resulted from the gap between the thermal expansion coefficients of celadon glaze and white slip.[36]

The gold-painted celadon wares of 13th century Goryeo and 12th century Northern Song were both low-fired at temperatures of 700-800 degrees Celsius after applying gold on glaze surfaces. But they differed in detailed methods of decoration. At the Ding kilns in 12th century China, gold was applied on a design pattern on the glaze surface and then the pattern was removed before firing. Through the method the decorative designs could be stylized and the brilliance of gold fully emphasized. In Goryeo, gold was applied to supplement inlaid designs and the smooth brushed lines could precisely express the smallest details.[37] Considering these technical as well as periodic differences, it is difficult to determine the relationship between the two methods.

34. Gold-painted design on the side of the flattened jar

Site of Hyeeumwon, House of Virtuous Grace

Goryeo built a state facility for travelers, named Hyeeumwon,[38] in Bong-seong County, which is present-day Yongmi 4-ri, Gwangtan-myeon, Paju City, Gyeonggi Province, a spot between the capital, Gaegyeong, and Nam-gyeong, the Southern Capital, which is today's Seoul. According to "Record on the Founding of Hyeeumsa," contained in *Anthology of Korean Literature* (*Dongmunseon*), compiled in 1478, the government of Goryeo began constructing a detached palace and a Buddhist chapel for the king, along with more lodging facilities, kitchens and warehouses for other travelers here in the eighth month of 1119, in accordance with a suggestion from Yi So-cheon. The construction was completed in the second month of 1120. King Injong (r. 1122-1146) named it Hyeeumsa, meaning the "temple of virtuous grace," after he ascended to the throne.

The state temple and travelers' house faced difficulties in operation amid the indifference of the central government when social chaos increased due to rebellions by powerful aristocrats and Buddhist monks, such as Yi Ja-gyeom and Myocheong. But it was greatly expanded and thrived again under the full patronage of King Injong and his wife, Queen Gongye. It was probably around this time that the renowned scholar-official Kim Bu-sik wrote "Record on the Founding of Hyeeumsa" (*Hyeeumsa sinchang gi*), dated 1144.[39] The remarkable quality as well as quantity of antique objects excavated from the site testifies to the authenticity of the record.

35. A general view of the site of Hyeeumwon

Excavated by the Buried Cultural Properties Research Institute of Dankook University in 2001-2004, and the HanBaek Research Institute for Cultural Heritage in 2008

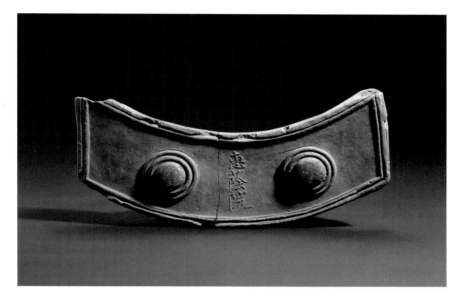

36. A concave roof-end tile inscribed with "Hyeeumwon"

Goryeo, first half of the 12th century to the first half of the 13th century
Excavated from Hyeeumwon site
H. 9.1cm, W. 27.5cm
Excavated by the Buried Cultural Properties Research Institute of Dankook University

The ruins of Hyeeumwon have yielded a broad variety of relics, including ceramics, roof tiles, earthenware and metal objects. The ceramics found here are mostly Goryeo celadon, Goryeo white porcelain, *buncheong* ware, Joseon white porcelain, and Chinese imports. Among these, celadon wares of Goryeo certainly draw the greatest attention.

The Goryeo celadon vessels unearthed from the Hyeeumwon site are neatly formed with carefully selected clay, and coated with high quality glazes. Mostly saggar-covered or individually fired, they also have fine silica supports on the bases. Obviously, they were products of the royal kilns of Sadang-ri in Gangjin and Yucheon-ri in Buan, and supplied to the state facility under royal patronage.

White porcelain wares unearthed here are notably inferior in both quality and quantity when compared with celadon finds. Considering the Sadang-ri and Yucheon-ri kilns produced white porcelain as well as celadon, Hyeeumwon apparently used low quality white wares from other kilns while it used top quality celadon from the royal kilns. It leads to the assumption that the top quality celadon and low quality white porcelains were probably used by people of different classes. Another interesting fact is that, among the Chinese vessels found here, there are far more high quality porcelains than celadon wares. This implies that the upper-class celadon users of Goryeo preferred Chinese white wares to locally produced porcelains.

Top quality celadon as well as foreign imported wares were used at Hyeeumwon because it included a detached place where the Goryeo kings stayed during their tours to the Southern Capital.

37. Roof ridge end tile shaped like a dragon head

Goryeo, first half of the 12th century to the first half of the 13th century
Excavated from Hyeeumwon site
H. 28cm
Excavated by the Buried Cultural Properties Research Institute of Dankook University

38. Celadon lids

Goryeo, 12th century
Excavated from Hyeeumwon site
Right: H. 2.7cm
Excavated by the Buried Cultural Properties
Research Institute of Dankook University

Most of the celadon lids unearthed from Hyeeumwon site are cup covers with knobs at the center on the top. The majority of the lids are undecorated, but some have incised lines around the knob, which resemble foliate patterns. There also is a cover with a cross-shaped knob. An incense burner cover is assumed to have had an ornamental knob in a molded form.

39. Celadon bowls

Goryeo, 12th century
Excavated from Hyeeumwon site
Left: H. 6.8cm, D. 19.7cm (rim)
Excavated by the Buried Cultural Properties
Research Institute of Dankook University

Hyeeumwon site yielded celadon bowls decorated with various designs, which are mostly carved or incised. Among frequently found motifs are peony blossoms and scrolls, sunset hibiscus flowers, grapevines, young boy figures and parrots. Most bowls are high quality saggar-fired wares with silica supports.

40. Celadon cups

Goryeo, first half of the 12th century to the first half of the 13th century
Excavated from Hyeeumwon site
Far left: H. 4.3cm, D. 8.6cm (rim), 3.6cm (base)
Far right: H. 7.3cm, D. 8cm (rim), 5cm (base)
Excavated by the Buried Cultural Properties Research Institute of Dankook University

41. Celadon dishes

Goryeo, first half of the 12th century to the first half of the 13th century
Excavated from Hyeeumwon site
Far left: H. 3.4cm, D. 13cm (rim), 6.8cm (base)
Far right: H. 2.3cm, D. 10cm (rim), 8.2cm (base)
Excavated by the Buried Cultural Properties Research Institute of Dankook University

42. Celadon pillow with incised lotus design

Goryeo, 12th century
Excavated from Hyeeumwon site
Present L. 26.6cm, Present W. 10.5cm
Excavated by the Buried Cultural Properties Research
Institute of Dankook University

This celadon pillow has a neatly incised design of fully opened lotus flowers under a fine glaze in jade color from its peak years. The scroll bands along the borders are reminiscent of roof-end tiles unearthed from Sadang-ri kiln sites. Hyeeumwon site yielded two other celadon pillows, incised with frets and chrysanthemum scrolls respectively.

43. Celadon lotus-shaped incense burner

Goryeo, 12th century
Excavated from Hyeeumwon site
Present H. 9.6cm
Excavated by the HanBaek Research Institute for Cultural Heritage

44. Celadon incense burners

Goryeo, first half of the 12th century to the first half of the 13th century
Excavated from Hyeeumwon site
Left: H. 12cm
Right: Present H. 7.4cm
Excavated by the Buried Cultural Properties Research Institute of Dankook University .

45. Fragments of celadon plates with inlaid willow and waterfowl

Goryeo, 12th century to the first half of the 13th century
Excavated from Hyeeumwon site
Left: Present L. 10.3cm
Right: Present L. 15.3cm
Excavated by the Buried Cultural Properties
Research Institute of Dankook University

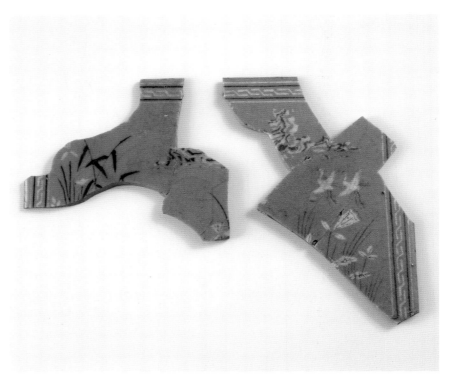

These are parts of a celadon plate, which is generally believed to have been used as a decorative tile. It is some 0.5-0.7 centimeters thick. The glazed outer surface has an inlaid design of lyrical waterside scenery with flying cranes, while the inside is unglazed. Similar celadon shards have been found at Yucheon-ri kiln sites.

46. Celadon shard with a molded toad

Goryeo, 12th century
Excavated from Hyeeumwon site
Present L. 5cm
Excavated by the Buried Cultural Properties
Research Institute of Dankook University

47. Fragments of Ding white porcelain and Jingdezhen bluish white porcelain

Song Dynasty of China
Excavated from Hyeeumwon site
Left middle row: H. 7.3cm, D. 10.5cm (rim), 6cm (base)
Right: H. 5.2cm, D. 18.2cm (rim), 5.6cm (base)
Excavated by the Buried Cultural Properties Research Institute of Dankook University

48. Fragments of celadon, and green-glazed and marble-patterned ceramics

Song Dynasty of China
Excavated from Hyeeumwon site
Front row left: Present H. 2.3cm
Back row right: Present H. 4cm
Excavated by the Buried Cultural Properties Research Institute of Dankook University

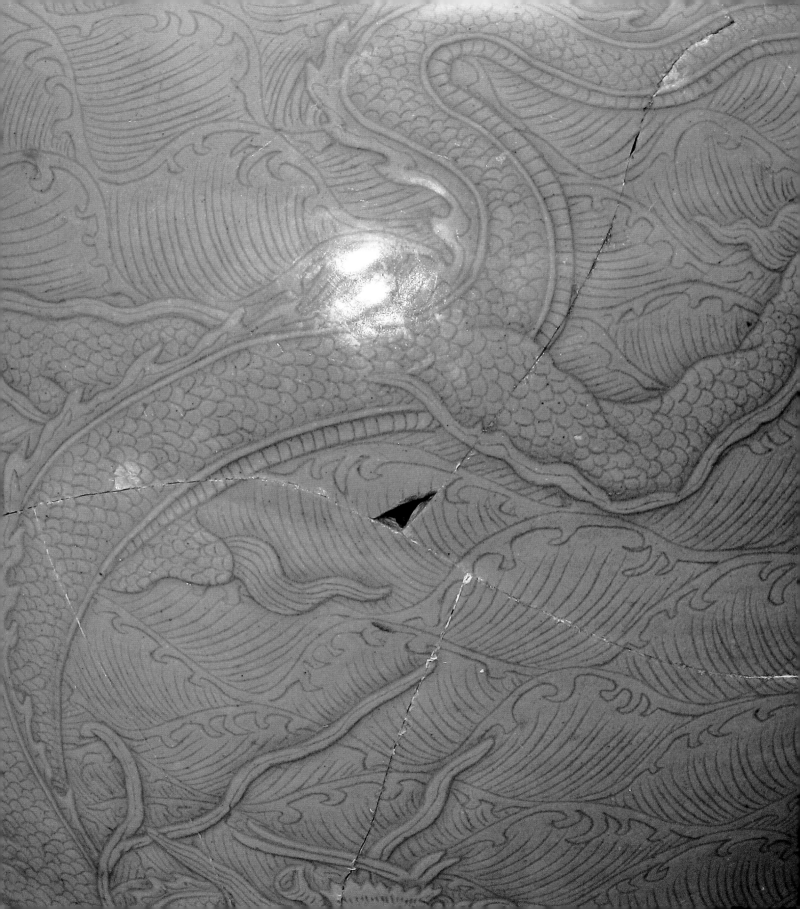

51. Broken celadon pillow with incised dragon design

Goryeo, 12th century
Excavated from a kiln site at Sadang-ri
H. 10.6cm, L. 21cm (the longest part), W. 15.2cm (the widest part)
National Museum of Korea

52. Broken celadon plum vase with carved lotus and sunset hibiscus design

Goryeo, 12th century
Excavated from a kiln site at Sadang-ri
Present H. 31.5cm, D. 14.5cm (base)
National Museum of Korea

53. Celadon shards decorated with peonies

Goryeo, 12th century
Excavated from kiln sites at Sadang-ri
Front row left: H. 5.5cm, D. 3.7cm (base)
Back row right: H. 4.7cm, D. 6.3cm (base)
National Museum of Korea

54. Fragments of celadon chairs with openwork decoration

Goryeo, 12th century
Excavated from kiln sites at Sadang-ri
Back row: Present H. 20.5cm, T. 1.5-2cm
National Museum of Korea

55. Shards of celadon incense burners with carved dragon design

Goryeo, 12th century
Excavated from kiln sites at Sadang-ri
Right: Present H. 11.6cm, Present W. 11.4cm
National Museum of Korea

56. Fragments of celadon with underglaze iron painting or iron glaze

Goryeo, 12th century
Excavated from kiln sites at Sadang-ri
Left: Present L. 11.7cm; Center: Present H. 14.7cm; Right (lid): H. 3.8cm, D. 9.7cm (the widest part)
National Museum of Korea

Kiln Sites in Buan

Celadon and porcelain vessels manufactured in Buan, North Jeolla Province, were notably lavish and decorative. Most pottery kilns here were clustered in two areas of Yucheon-ri and Jinseo-ri, and products from the former were generally more refined in style than those from the latter.[42] The difference could have been due to a time interval or a discontinuity in quality among contemporary kilns.

Many kiln sites in Buan were looted and excavated artifacts were smuggled out during the early 20th century. Presently, the National Museum of Korea and Ewha Womans University Museum have the largest amounts of relics excavated from Buan kiln sites.[43] Those at the National Museum of Korea were mostly unearthed from Yucheon-ri during the 1960s and some were donated by Lee Hong-kun (1900-1980, pen name Dongwon). Most artifacts excavated during the 1990s are kept at the Jeonju National Museum and the Wonkwang University Museum.

Buan kiln sites were first surveyed by the Japanese in 1928,[44] and later by several Korean organizations.[45] As a result, kiln sites at Yucheon-ri were designated as Historic Site No. 69, and those at Jinseo-ri as Historic Site No. 70.

Thirty-seven kiln sites have been identified so far in Yucheon-ri and some 40 in Jinseo-ri, mostly clustered around hilly areas. All are "climbing kilns," built on slopes. In 1997, an excavation team of Wonkwang University Museum confirmed five kiln sites, of which Kiln No. 5 was discovered in the best condition. This kiln is presumed to have been some 15.5 meters long.

57. A view of a pottery kiln site at Yucheon-ri, Buan County

A glass negative made before 1945
National Museum of Korea

Everyday wares such as bowls, dishes and cups were found in large quantities from kiln ruins and sedimentary layers in Buan. Various pottery making tools, including saggars and firing stands, were also discovered.

What is particularly remarkable about celadon pieces unearthed from Yucheon-ri sites is that they include objects in the same styles as royal wares of Goryeo. For example, they show marked stylistic resemblance to celadon objects found in Jireung, the tomb of King Myeongjong (r. 1170-1197); Seongneung, the tomb of King Huijong (r. 1204-1211); and ruins of Hyeeumwon, a detached palace in Paju, built in 1122.[46] They strongly attest to the close relationship between Yucheon-ri kilns and pottery wares used by the Goryeo royal families.

Among celadon objects discovered in the tomb of King Myeongjong, two bowls are especially similar in style to Yucheon-ri ware. One has inlaid litchi scrolls and the other has a cloud and crane design (Plates 17, 18). Particularly, the bowl with litchi scrolls is exactly identical in style with Yucheon-ri ware: it has litchi scrolls inlaid with even intervals on the interior and more scrolls rendered in reverse inlay inside double concentric circles on the exterior. The vessel form and glaze are also markedly similar. Seongneung, the tomb of King Huijong, also yielded a celadon dish with underglaze iron painting, which closely echoes Yucheon-ri ware (Plate 23). Ruins of Hyeeumwon have also yielded a number of celadon pieces that strongly suggest they were shipped from Yucheon-ri. A celadon multi-sided dish with floral design (Plate 41) particularly shows stylistic affinities to celadon shards unearthed from Yucheon-ri. They draw even greater attention as Jireung, the tomb of King Myeongjong, was found to have contained an unmistakable stylistic cousin (Plate 19).

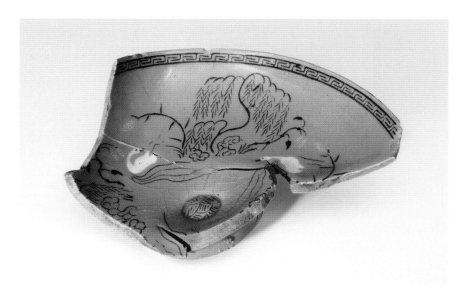

58. Celadon bowl with inlaid willow, reed and waterfowl

Goryeo, second half of the 12th century to 13th century
Excavated from a kiln site at Yucheon-ri
Donated by Lee Hong-kun
Present H. 5.2cm, D. 4.7cm (base)
National Museum of Korea

59. Celadon incense burner with carved willow, reed and waterfowl

Goryeo, second half of the 12th century to 13th century
Excavated from a kiln site at Yucheon-ri
Donated by Lee Hong-kun
H. 12.7cm, W. 27cm (the widest part)
National Museum of Korea

60. Fragments of a celadon plum vase with inlaid oddly-shaped rocks and waterfowl

Goryeo, second half of the 12th century to 13th century
Excavated from a kiln site at Yucheon-ri
Donated by Lee Hong-kun
Present H. 20.2cm
National Museum of Korea

61. Fragments of a celadon plum vase with inlaid sunset hibiscus

Goryeo, second half of the 12th century to 13th century
Excavated from a kiln site at Yucheon-ri
Donated by Lee Hong-kun
Present H. 24.7cm
National Museum of Korea

62. Celadon pillow with inlaid clouds and cranes

Goryeo, second half of the 12th century to 13th century
Excavated from a kiln site at Yucheon-ri
Donated by Lee Hong-kun
H. 11.1cm, L. 29.4cm (the longest part)
National Museum of Korea

63. Celadon shards with inlaid landscape

Goryeo, second half of the 12th century to 13th century
Excavated from a kiln site at Yucheon-ri
Donated by Lee Hong-kun
Left: Present L. 12.3cm, Present W. 12.8cm
National Museum of Korea

64. Celadon vessel covers

Goryeo, second half of the 12th century to 13th century
Excavated from kiln sites at Yucheon-ri
Donated by Lee Hong-kun
Left: H. 3.9cm
Right: H. 3.8cm, D. 12.5cm
National Museum of Korea

65. Broken celadon cups and stands

Goryeo, second half of the 12th century to
13th century
Excavated from kiln sites at Yucheon-ri
Donated by Lee Hong-kun
Left on the back row: H. 7.4cm, D. 8.2cm (base),
16.2cm (the widest part)
National Museum of Korea

▽ 66. Broken celadon dishes with inlaid floral designs

Goryeo, second half of the 12th century to
13th century
Excavated from kiln sites at Yucheon-ri
Donated by Lee Hong-kun
Left on the front row: H. 2.5cm, D. 11.4cm (rim), 7cm
(base); Left on the back row: H. 6.4cm
National Museum of Korea

67. Celadon plum vase with inlaid plantain and toads

Goryeo, second half of the 12th century to 13th century
Excavated from a kiln site at Yucheon-ri
Donated by Lee Hong-kun
Present H. 30.8cm
National Museum of Korea

68. Celadon bottle with inlaid lotus and chrysanthemum

Goryeo, second half of the 12th century to
13th century
Excavated from a kiln site at Yucheon-ri
Donated by Lee Hong-kun
H. 34.7cm
National Museum of Korea

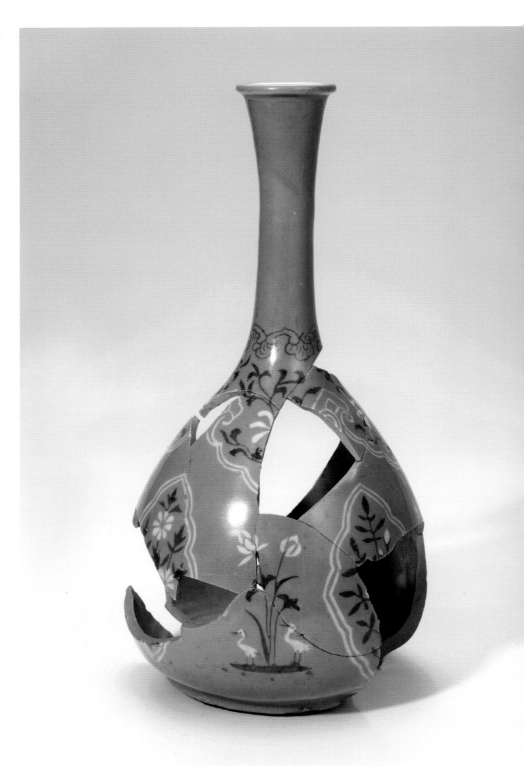

69. Porcelain shards

Goryeo, second half of the 12th century to 13th century
Excavated from Kiln Site No. 12 at Yucheon-ri
Right on the back row (incense burner): Present H. 8.5cm, D. 11.5cm (base)
National Museum of Korea

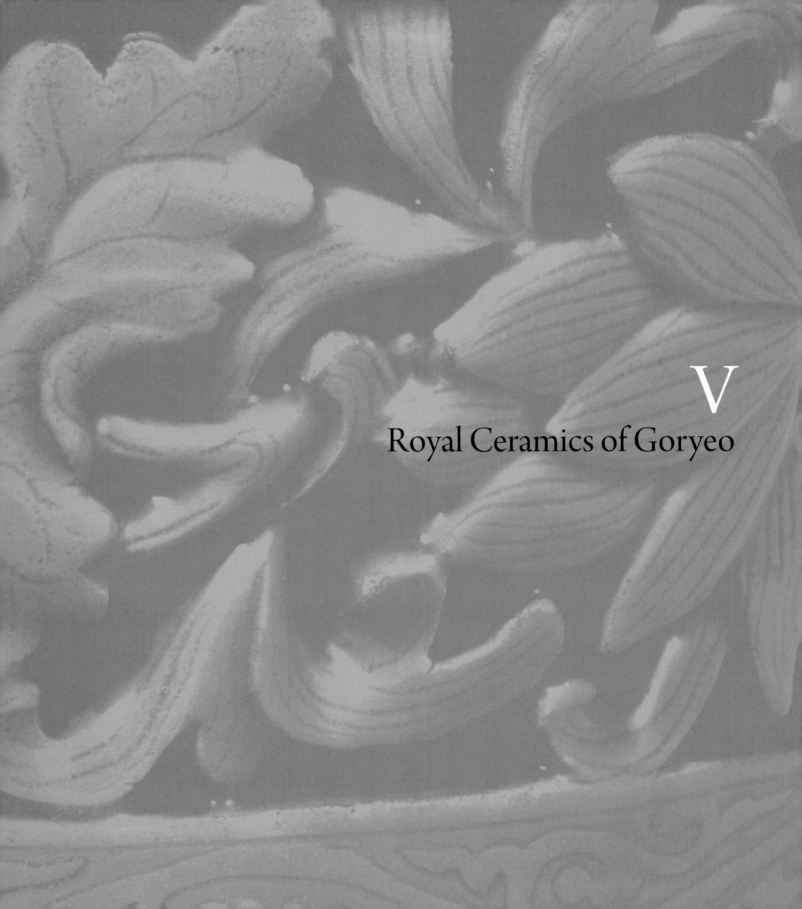

V

Royal Ceramics of Goryeo

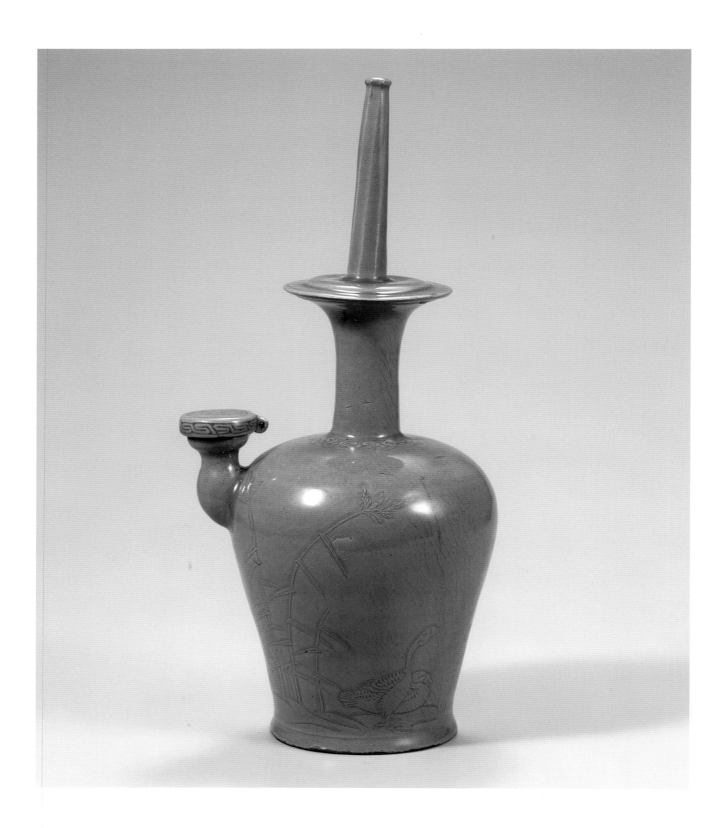

70. Celadon ritual ewer carved with willow, reed and waterfowl

Goryeo, 12th century
Excavated in Gaeseong
Treasure No. 344
H. 34.2cm, D. 9.3cm (base)
National Museum of Korea

Ritual ewers, or kundika, were introduced from India through China along with Buddhism. In Goryeo these ritual bottles were first made with metal but celadon ewers followed thanks to advances in pottery-making skills. They were used to offer holy water at temple altars and regarded as a symbol of Avalokitesvara, the Bodhisattva of Compassion, as shown in many Buddhist paintings of the Goryeo period. In his travel record, *Illustrated Account of Goryeo* (*Xuanhe fengshi gaoli tujing*), the Song diplomat Xu Jing wrote that these celadon bottles were "widely used by the nobility and at government offices, temples and private households but simply to hold water." This implies that they were also used as everyday vessels during the first half of the 12th century.

This celadon ewer is carved with reeds and a pair of wild geese on the front and a pair of mandarin ducks resting under a willow tree on the back. A sand dune and water grass are expressed on a line incised above the base to create lyrical waterside scenery. A mandarin duck swims creating waves on the opposite side of the spout, which is apparently a scheme to make the undecorated space seen as the surface of water. The neck and the lid have small decorative patterns.

The ewer closely resembles a bronze kundika designated National Treasure No. 92 in shape and decoration. The bronze ewer also has willow, reed and waterfowl but inlaid with silver wire. It shows how metal ware influenced celadon production.

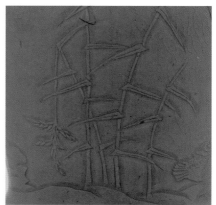

71. Celadon plum vase with incised lotus scrolls

Goryeo, 12th century
National Treasure No. 97
H. 43.9cm, D. 7.2cm (rim), 15.8cm (base)
National Museum of Korea

This elegant celadon vase epitomizes the high standards of aestheticism pursued by people of Goryeo in the 12th century. It has an overall design of large lotus flowers and scrolls, skillfully incised by slanting the carving knife. The relatively broad and deep incisions create semi-relief effects, while the petals and leaves are precisely expressed with fine lines.

Creating semi-relief effects by incising with a slanted knife was a popular technique frequently employed at the Yaozhou and Ding kilns in China during the Northern Song period. Owing to this technique, Goryeo celadon attained much gentler impressions as sharp lines increasingly became smoother. It was also a useful technique for highlighting the primary motif in a multi-motif pattern. Celadon shards with similar characteristics as this vase have been unearthed from kiln sites at Yongun-ri and Sadang-ri in Gangjin.

72. Fragments of celadon plum vases

Excavated from kiln sites at Sadang-ri
Left: Present H. 8.5cm, D. 6.4cm (rim)
Right: Present H. 17.8cm
National Museum of Korea

73. Celadon plum vase with carved peony scrolls and dragons

Goryeo, 12th century
Excavated in Gaeseong
H. 37.9 cm, D. 6.1cm (rim), 11.7cm (base)
National Museum of Korea

This plum vase, or *maebyeong* (*meiping* in Chinese), has eight foliated panels around its streamlined body, each carved with a dragon ascending to heaven. The background is carved with peony scrolls, with the shoulder and the base surrounded with lotus bands. The carving was done very carefully, sometimes by slanting the knife to express delicate contours. Fragments of a celadon plum vase with identical characteristics were discovered from a kiln site at Sadang-ri in Gangjin

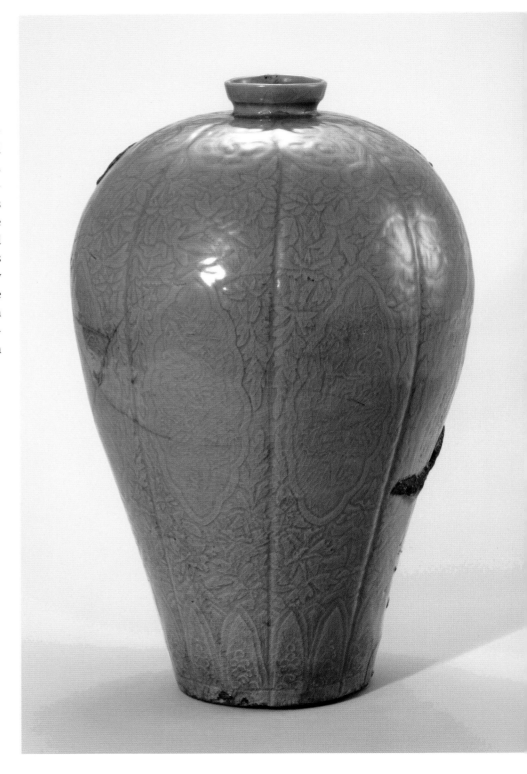

74. Celadon pomegranate and monkey-shaped water dropper

Goryeo, 12th century
Excavated in Gaeseong
H. 8cm, D. 7.9cm
National Museum of Korea

75. Celadon turtle-shaped water dropper with dragon head

Goryeo, 12th century
Excavated in Gaeseong
H. 6.1cm
National Museum of Korea

76. Celadon monkey-shaped ink jar

Goryeo, 12th century
Excavated in Gaeseong
H. 7.1cm
National Museum of Korea

This amusing ink jar is a good example of Goryeo celadon that delights the viewer with unexpected ingenuity. The small vessel is in the shape of a monkey holding up a jar; the monkey, wearing a bell around its neck, is skillfully expressed in minute details, such as tiny little strands of fur. With a lovely facial expression, it seems like a smart and witty creature.

Not many Goryeo celadon objects were sculpted in the form of a monkey, but a few existing examples are all charming works of art. A pomegranate-shaped water dropper decorated with a monkey (Plate 74) at the National Museum of Korea and a water dropper in the shape of mother and baby monkeys at the Kansong Art Museum are the two most well-known pieces. The latter is particularly famous; it expresses a mother monkey tenderly embracing her baby. Monkeys depicted by Goryeo potters usually have pleasant impressions.

77. Celadon brush stand with dragon heads and openwork lotus scrolls

Goryeo, 12th century
Excavated in Gaeseong
H. 9cm, L. 17.4cm, W. 4.8cm
National Museum of Korea

Few celadon brush stands of the Goryeo period remain today and those decorated with skillful openwork designs like this one are even rarer. A variety of decorative techniques, such as molding, openwork, incising, carving and underglaze iron ornament, were adroitly harmonized to create a small but beautiful piece. The dragon heads on both ends of the rectangular stand look lively, with the canine teeth and scales ornately carved and the eyes marked with iron dots. It shows the high standard of Goryeo celadon during its peak years in the 12th century.

78. Celadon turtle-shaped ewer with dragon head

Goryeo, 12th century
Excavated in Gaeseong; National Treasure No. 96; H. 17.3cm
National Museum of Korea

This celadon ewer is shaped like a turtle sitting on a lotus stand, but the spout is in the shape of a dragon head. This was probably inspired by turtle-shaped pedestals for tomb steles of Goryeo, which often had a dragon head. The dragon has whiskers, teeth, scales, horns and mane, all finely carved. The eyes are expressed with underglaze iron dots. Each hexagon of the shell is engraved with the Chinese character *wang*, meaning the "king," suggesting the status of the person who used the ewer.

79. Celadon dragon-shaped ewer

Goryeo, 12th century
Excavated in Gaeseong
National Treasure No. 61
H. 24.4cm, D. 10.3cm (base)
National Museum of Korea

This celadon ewer is in the shape of an animal with a dragon head and fish body. With its fins spread and tail held up, the animal is reminiscent of a dragon soaring up vigorously from water. Characterized by dynamic form and lustrous glaze, the ewer represents the apex of Goryeo celadon making skill in the 12th century. The imaginary animal was believed to possess the power to chase away evil spirits. Hence it was often used on buildings.[47] Decorative roof tiles bearing similar designs have been found at the ruins of Hyeeumwon, a detached palace in Paju,[48] as well as the royal palace site in Gaeseong, the old capital of Goryeo.[49]

80. Celadon foliated dishes

Goryeo, 12th century
Excavated in Gaeseong
H. 3.6cm, D. 17.6cm
National Museum of Korea

81. Celadon foliated cup stand

Goryeo, 12th century
H. 6.7cm
National Museum of Korea

82. Celadon lotus-shaped incense burner

Goryeo, 12th century
Excavated in Gaeseong
H. 15.2cm, D. 10.5cm (rim)
National Museum of Korea

This incense burner consists of three parts -- a burner shaped like a lotus flower, a base shaped like an inverted lotus flower and a plate inserted in between. Its form echoes a gilt silver incense burner excavated from the underground palace of Famen temple in Xi'an, China. The ninth century Tang piece has an openwork cover designed to puff out smoke.

Incense burners in this Tang original style continued to be made until the Southern Song period, though varying in details according to times.[50] Particularly, a celadon lotus-shaped incense burner discovered from the ruins of Ru kiln at Qingliang temple of the Northern Song period has a very similar form to Goryeo wares, proving Xu Jing's remarks on the intimate relationship between Ru ware and Goryeo celadon. The incense burners of Goryeo were evidently modeled after earlier Chinese examples, especially under the influence of Ru ware.[51]

Incense burners in this type have been excavated from Goryeo kiln sites at Sadang-ri and Samheung-ri in Daegu-myeon, Gangjin County, and Yucheon-ri in Boan-myeon, Buan County, as well as the ruins of Hyeeumwon, a detached palace in Paju. They all have bases shaped like an inverted lotus flower, but some of them have a bead protruding from each petal. Also, some of the plates connecting the burner and the base have handles shaped like a dragon head, while others are simply carved with scroll patterns.

A fragment of a lotus-shaped celadon incense burner excavated from a Yucheon-ri kiln site, kept at the National Museum of Korea, has lotus petals with blunt contours but finely incised veins. This is a fresh attempt not found in Ru ware. It implies that Goryeo celadon began to develop its own characteristics after faithfully following Chinese styles.

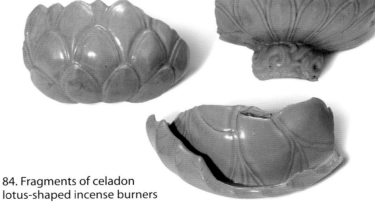

▽83. Fragment of a celadon lotus-shaped incense burner

Excavated from a kiln site at Yucheon-ri
Donated by Lee Hong-kun
Present H. 8cm, W. 19.3cm
National Museum of Korea

84. Fragments of celadon lotus-shaped incense burners

Excavated from kiln sites at Sadang-ri
Right on the back row: Present H. 9.8cm, W. 15.8cm
National Museum of Korea

85. Celadon incense burner with dragon-shaped cover

Goryeo, 12th century
Excavated in Gaeseong
H. 22.7cm
National Museum of Korea

Celadon incense burners of Goryeo were basically modeled after earlier metal prototypes. But potters took advantage of the soft and elastic property of clay to decorate their wares with carvings and sculpted forms.

This round incense burner with a broad rim is supported by three legs in the form of animal heads. It is designed to allow the smoke of burning incense to be emitted through the mouth of a dragon crouching on the cover. The covers of celadon incense burners of Goryeo were usually surmounted by ornaments in animal forms, including real animals such as ducks and mandarin ducks, and imaginary animals such as dragons, mythical unicorns or the dharma-protecting lions.

In China, incense burners with similar features are found among celadon of Yaozhou and *qingbai* (bluish white) ware of Jingdezhen of Northern Song from the latter half of the 11th century as well as celadon made at Ru kilns during the 12th century. In Korea, kiln site excavations have confirmed production of celadon incense burners in this type at Kiln Site No. 10 in Yongun-ri,[52] and Sadang-ri and Samheung-ri[53] in Gangjin, and Yucheon-ri in Buan. Though its cover is missing, a similar incense burner was also found in Golleung, the tomb of Queen Dowager Wondeok (?-1239). It is assumed that incense burners in this type appeared around the mid-11th century,[54] and continued to be made until the early half of the 13th century.

The cover of this incense burner is embellished with a sculpted dragon holding a treasure bead in its front paw. Similar celadon shards were found from the kiln site of Ru at Qingliang temple in China, supporting Xu Jing's comment on the relationship between China's Ru ware and Goryeo celadon.[55] Goryeo potters began to make celadon incense burners under Chinese influence,[56] but gradually achieved unique beauty of form and refined aestheticism.

86. Celadon incense burner with lion-shaped cover

Goryeo, 12th century
Excavated in Gaeseong
National Treasure No. 60
H. 21.2cm
National Museum of Korea

The Chinese envoy Xu Jing, who visited Gaegyeong, present-day Gaeseong, in 1123, wrote in his often quoted book, *Illustrated Account of Goryeo* (*Xuanhe fengshi gaoli tujing*) : "A lion (*suani*) emits incense and is likewise 'kingfisher colored': the beast crouches on the top, supported by a lotus. This is the most distinguished of all their wares." The scholar diplomat was in the Goryeo capital in the first year of the reign of King Injong.

This incense burner consists of a round body with a broad rim and a cover surmounted by a sculpted lion. It is supported by three legs in the form of animal heads, not a lotus as described by Xu Jing, but it still clearly shows the style of Goryeo celadon during the first half of the 12th century. Celadon shards in the same style have been excavated from kiln sites at Sadang-ri and Samheung-ri in Gangjin, and Yucheon-ri in Buan. A tripod incense burner with legs in the form of animal head was also found in Golleung, the tomb of Queen Dowager Wondeok (?-1239). Although this incense burner was found without a cover, it seems obvious that celadon incense burners with

covers decorated with sculpted animals were made during the first half of the 13th century.

Xu also noted that metal incense burners decorated with sculpted animal figures were used to burn incense for official palace events. Given the symbolism of the lion as a dharma protector and the devout faith in Buddhism of the ruling elite of Goryeo, celadon incense burners with sculpted lions were probably used at Buddhist events.

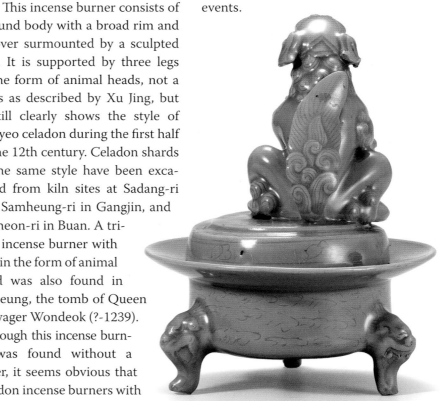

87. Celadon incense burner with openwork decoration

Goryeo, 12th century
Excavated in Gaeseong
National Treasure No. 95
H. 15.3cm (total), D. 11.5cm
National Museum of Korea

This beautiful incense burner represents the aesthetic excellence of Goryeo celadon and has been displayed in many overseas exhibitions. It is an exquisite piece of art that looks as if it is carved out of jade rather than a ceramic object. It is gorgeously decorated without losing balance and exerts graceful dignity.

The incense burner consists of three parts – a body for burning incense, a cover for emitting smoke and a stand. The cover is surmounted with a ball of openwork design so the smoke can be released through the perforations. The ball has an openwork design of overlapped loops, which were considered coins standing for happiness, one of the traditional seven treasures. But similar balls have been found on a bronze seal excavated from the tomb of King Injong (Plate 8) and another celadon incense burner (Plate 85), both held by lions, the dharma protector. Hence it is likely that the ball on this incense burner is also a treasure bead symbolizing the law and virtue of the Buddha.

The body is covered with lotus petals individually sculpted and appliquéd. The same technique was employed for the petals joining the body and the stand. Three cute rab-

bits support the incense burner. It is wondrous that the tiny figures look strong enough to bear the weight and maintain balance as they succinctly express the character of rabbits.

This incense burner is a notable accomplishment in that it adroitly harmonizes different forms and functions of three components. Also remarkable is the combination of various decorative techniques, including incising, carving, openwork, inlay and appliqué.

88. Celadon incense burner with impressed monsters

Goryeo, 12th century
H. 11.1cm, L. 14.1cm, W. 12.7cm
National Museum of Korea

Goryeo potters made celadon incense burners modeled after ancient Chinese bronzes. These incense burners in *ding* style are divided into two types -- round or rectangular.

This incense burner in a rectangular *ding* type was formed by joining rectangular clay plates. It has vertical square handles and short legs with elephant eyes. The sides are divided into two levels; the narrow upper level has designs of a legendary bird, called *kuifeng*, impressed in relief on a background with fret patterns, and the lower level has mythical monster designs, called *taotie*, also impressed in relief against fret patterns. Celadon shards showing the same features were unearthed from Level II of Kiln Site No. 10 at Yongun-ri as well as Sadang-ri sites in Gangjin.

89. Celadon incense burner with impressed monsters

Goryeo, 12th century
Excavated in Gaeseong; H. 13.3cm, D. 11.7cm (rim)
National Museum of Korea

Celadon production in Goryeo came under the influence of ancient Chinese bronzes as the royal court of Goryeo adopted the ritual system of the Song Dynasty. Goryeo based its ritual protocols on the Song system and also adopted Chinese-style ritual vessels. Potters of Goryeo formed their wares by referring to Chinese bronze styles learned from books such as *Catalogue of Antiquities* (*Xuanhe bogutu*), which introduced the vast antique collection of Emperor Huizong (1082-1135).[57]

This round incense burner has three short legs and two vertical loop handles. It has fret patterns impressed all over the exterior, which is divided into two levels. The upper level has legendary bird designs, called *kuifeng* and the lower level has mythical monsters, called *taotie*. Celadon shards showing the same techniques and motifs have been found at Sadang-ri kiln sites.

90. Fragment of a celadon incense burner with impressed monsters

Excavated from a kiln site at Sadang-ri
Present H. 13.5cm
National Museum of Korea

91. Celadon bowl carved with lotus pond and children

Goryeo, 12th century
Excavated in Gaeseong
H. 5.6cm, D. 18.1cm (rim)
National Museum of Korea

92. Celadon pillow with openwork
lotus scrolls

Goryeo, 12th century
Excavated in Gaeseong
H. 11.2cm, W. 26.7cm
National Museum of Korea

93. Celadon bowl with inlaid floral scrolls

Goryeo, *circa* 1159
Excavated from the tomb of Mun Gong-yu(?-1159) in Gaepung County, Gyeonggi Province
National Treasure No. 115
H. 6.2cm, D. 16.8cm (rim), 4.4cm (base)
National Museum of Korea

This tea bowl with a pure jade glaze and a tomb plate were excavated from the tomb of Mun Gong-yu, who died in 1159. It is the oldest known celadon piece with a clear date and a crucial object for charting the evolution of Goryeo celadon. With both incised and inlaid patterns, the bowl is regarded to show a transition from the early engraving technique to inlaying.

According to the tomb plate, Mun Gong-yu served the court of King Injong (r. 1122-1146) as a civil official reputed for his academic and artistic achievements. He might have used the bowl, or perhaps it was made after his death as a funerary gift. It is also possible that the bowl was a gift from the royal court because tea bowls with similar features were produced at the royal kilns in Gangjin and Buan and have been found at the palace site in Gaeseong.

The fact that a high quality tea bowl was buried in the grave of an aristocrat is evidence that tea drinking was part of upper-class culture in Goryeo. Tea was introduced to Korea during Unified Silla and widely enjoyed in Goryeo. According to *History of Goryeo* (*Goryeo sa*) and *Essentials of Goryeo History* (*Goryeo sa jeoryo*), the government of Goryeo had an office named the Chamber of Tea (*Dabang*), which was responsible for preparing tea for official events of the state and the court as well as daily tea drinking in the palace. Goryeo royal family and nobility enjoyed powder tea, which was made by grinding a tea brick on a stone and adding hot water. Tea bricks were made by grinding tea leaves into fine powder and compressing it in molds.

Celadon tea bowls of Goryeo reflect the refined aesthetic tastes of Goryeo people, who enjoyed drinking tea along with the visual pleasure it provided. Tea bowls were decorated with various patterns. The rapidly widening, straight vessel wall of this bowl was for enjoying the froth and grounds of tea together.

94. Celadon plum vase with inlaid bamboo and cranes

Goryeo, second half of the 12th century to 13th century
Treasure No. 903
H. 38.9cm, D. 5.1cm (rim)
Private collection

While plain celadon is prized for glazes in deep bluish green jade colors, inlaid celadon pleases the viewer with a variety of charming decorative patterns. Looking at Goryeo celadon, one can indirectly experience the emotional world and thinking of Goryeo people. In this context, this celadon plum vase naturally makes us wonder what kind of person its owner was. The graceful vase has a lyrical pattern succinctly harmonizing a generous space arrangement and exquisite inlaid patterns.

The vase gives one the feeling of strolling in a mysterious garden, where bamboo trees and plum blossoms create a picturesque scene and cranes slumber or fly around. Small cranes flying above the trees create a wonderful sense of distance and depth in a limited space. Bamboo and plum branches are inlaid in black and plum blossoms in white so finely and delicately that they look as if drawn with a brush. Celadon shards showing similar decorative schemes and techniques have been found mostly from kiln sites at Yucheon-ri in Buan.

95. Fragments of celadon plum vases with inlaid willow design

Excavated from kiln sites at Yucheon-ri
Donated by Lee Hong-kun
Left: Present H. 10.3cm
National Museum of Korea

96. Celadon gourd-shaped ewer with inlaid peony scrolls

Goryeo, second half of the 12th century to 13th century
National Treasure No. 116
H. 34.3cm, D. 2cm (rim), 9.7cm (base)
National Museum of Korea

97. Celadon plum vase with inlaid peony and underglaze copper-red decoration

Goryeo, second half of the 12th century to
13th century
Excavated in Gaeseong
Treasure No. 346
H. 34.5cm, D. 5.8cm (rim), 13.2cm (base)
National Museum of Korea

Appendices

Notes

I. History of Goryeo Royal Ceramics

1) Lan Pu, *Yeokju gyeongdeokjin dorok* ("*Annotated Pottery Records of Jingdezhen*"), compiled by Zheng Yangui, and translated and annotated by Lim Sang-yeol (Seoul: Iljisa, 2004); Book VII "Ancient Kilns," Appendix: "Kilns of Goryeo."

II. Ceramics from Goryeo Royal Tombs

2) Xu Jing, *Xuanhe fengshi gaoli tujing* ("*Illustrated Account of Goryeo*"), Book 2 "Genealogy."

3) Jeong In-ji et al, *Goryeo sa* ("*History of Goryeo*"), Book 17 "Powerful Families," Chapter 17 "Twenty-fourth Year of the Reign of King Injong."

4) Ryu Imanishi, "Report on Surveys of Goryeo Royal Tombs," *Survey Report on Historic Sites of the Fifth Year of Emperor Taisho* (Gyeongseong: Joseon (Korea) Government-General, 1916), p. 264.

5) The conservation science team of the National Museum of Korea conducted material analysis and conservation treatment on non-celadon objects excavated from King Injong's tomb. Survey results are partially introduced in this catalogue and will be fully published in a paper.

6) Through study of various catalogues and reports on artifacts excavated from King Injong's tomb and the Japanese colonial government's official documents on purchase of celadon objects, it was confirmed that the tomb yielded four celadon objects introduced in this catalogue. Their relic numbers are Main Hall 4254, 4255, 4256 and 4257. Most of the celadon pieces mistakenly identified as wares from King Injong's tomb were actually unearthed from other royal graves of Goryeo or around Gaeseong. They were purchased by or donated to the museum of the Japanese government-general between 1908 and 1916.

7) *China at the Inception of the Second Millennium A.D.- Art and Culture of the Sung Dynasty, 960-1279* (Taipei: National Palace Museum, 2000), pp. 98-99.

8) Xu Jing, *op. cit.* Book 11 "Honor Guards," translated by Jo Dong-won et al. (Seoul: Taurus Books, 2005), pp. 154-161.

9) Kim Woollim, "Heavenly Guardians from King Injong's Tomb and Academic Buddhist and Taoist Figure Painting Style in the mid-Goryeo Dynasty," *National Museum Journal of Arts 69* (Seoul: National Museum of Korea, 2003), pp. 58-61. (Kim pays attention to resemblances to Chinese Taoist paintings, stressing the significance of the guardian images on King Injong's epitaph as evidence of the influence of Taoist style of Northern Song court painters on Korean painting during the mid-Goryeo period.)

10) *Ganghwa Seongneung* (*Excavation Report for Seokneung(tomb) of Heuijong, the King of Goryeo Dynasty in Ganghwa Island, Incheon Metropolitan City*) (Daejeon: National Research Institute of Cultural Heritage, 2003), pp. 63-122.

11) *Goryeo sa* ("*History of Goryeo*"), Book 88 "Biographies," Chapter 1 "Queen Dowager Sungyeong, Lady Kim."

12) *Goryeo sa* ("*History of Goryeo*"), Book 28 "Powerful Families," Chapter 28 "First Year of the Reign of King Chungnyeol."

13) "Report on Surveys of Goryeo Royal Tombs" (*Survey Report on Historic Sites of the Fifth Year of Emperor Taisho),* published in 1916 by the Japanese colonial government, says the tomb is in Gareung-ri, Yangdo-myeon, Ganghwa County.

14) Ryu Imanishi, *op. cit.*, 1916, p. 420.

15) *Excavation Report on Goryeo Royal Tombs of Ganghwado* (Daejeon: National Research Institute of Cultural Heritage, 2007), pp. 60-98.

16) This jade ornament might have been brought from China as there are similar pieces dated to Jin and Yuan periods.

17) This table compares King Injong's epitaph book and the marble strips found in Gareung, or Queen Dowager Sungyeong's tomb:

(unit: cm)

	Total length	Thickness	Width	Distance from edge to holes	Diameter of holes
Epitaph book of King Injong	33	2.5	3	4.7-4.8	0.6-0.7
Marble strips of Gareung	·	1.4-1.8	2.8-2.9	4.8-4.9	0.5-0.6

18) Marble strips from Gareung, bearing no inscriptions, are assumed to be the concluding parts of an epitaph book. King Injong's epitaph book has empty space without lettering at the end, and the inscription runs 23.4 centimeters, with 4.7cm margins on the top and the bottom.

19) *Ibid.* (Daejeon: National Research Institute of Cultural Heritage, 2007), p. 69.

20) *Ibid.* (Daejeon: National Research Institute of Cultural Heritage, 2007), pp. 141-339.

21) *Ibid.* (Daejeon: National Research Institute of Cultural Heritage, 2007), pp. 359-407.

III. Goryeo Royal Ceramics from Other Historic Sites

22) *Goryeo sa* ("*History of Goryeo*"), Book 22 "Powerful Families," Chapter 22 "The Fourth Year of King Gojong" (1217); Book 26 "Powerful Families" Chapter 26 "The Ninth Year of King Wonjong" (1268); Book 29 "Powerful Families" Chapter 29 "The Ninth Year of King Chungnyeol" (1283); Book 46 "Powerful Families" Chapter 46 "The Fourth Year of King Gongyang" (1392); Book 70 "Records" Chapter 23 "Rites 11."

23) *Sinjeung dongguk yeoji seungnam* ("*Augmented Survey of the Geography of Korea*"), Book 5 "Gaeseong City Part 2."

24) Xu Jing, *op. cit.*, Book 5 "Royal Palace Part 1"; Xu Jing, *op. cit.*, translated by Jo Dong-won et al. (Seoul: Taurus Books, 2005), pp. 97-99.

25) The National Museum of Korea keeps documents about surface investigations conducted by the Japanese government-general as well as a celadon jar decorated with a monkey excavated from ruins of the royal palace of Goryeo in Gaeseong.

26) *Gaeseong Goryeo gungseong* (*Excavation Research Report of Goryeo Royal Palace of Kaesong*) (Daejeon: National Research Institute of Cultural Heritage, 2008), p. 1.

27) *Goryeo sa* ("*History of Goryeo*"), Book 18 "Powerful Families" Chapter 18 "The 19th Year of King Yejong" (1165); Book 18 "Powerful Families" Chapter 18 "The 21st Year of King Yejong" (1167).

28) *Goryeo sa* ("*History of Goryeo*"), Book 53 "Records" Chapter 1 "First of the Five Elements: Water."

29) Press release of the International Exchange Division of the Cultural Heritage Administration,

June 29, 2007; *Ibid.* (Daejeon: National Research Institute of Cultural Heritage, 2008).

30) "Two Celadon Pieces from Kiln Sites in Daegu-myeon," *Ceramics 6-6* (Tokyo: Oriental Ceramic Research Institute, 1934); Choi Sun-u, "Celadon Roof Tiles of Goryeo," *National Museum Journal of Arts 13* (Seoul: National Museum of Korea, 1969).

31) Choi Sun-u, "Celadon Roof Tiles Excavated from Kiln Sites at Sadang-ri, Gangjin," *National Museum Journal of Arts 9* (Seoul: National Museum of Korea, 1964), pp. 24-25; *op. cit.* (Seoul: National Museum of Korea, 1969), pp. 1-11.

32) *Goryeo sa* ("History of Goryeo"), Book 28 "Powerful Families" Chapter 28 "The First Year of King Chungnyeol"; Book 105 "Biographies" Chapter 18 "Jo In-gyu."

33) Ken Nomori, *Study of Goryeo Ceramics* (Kyoto: Seikansha, 1944), p. 62.

34) Kang Kyung-sook, *History of Korean Ceramics* (Seoul: Iljisa, 1989), p. 203.

35) Chung Yang-mo, *Museum News No. 11* (Seoul: National Museum of Korea, 1971), p. 3.

36) Hwang Hyun-Sung, "Scientific Survey on Gold Painting Techniques of Korean and Chinese Ceramics," *Chinese Ceramics at the National Museum of Korea* (Seoul: National Museum of Korea, 2007), p. 443.

37) Hwang Hyun-Sung, *op. cit.*, pp. 448-449.

38) The ruins of Hyeeumwon were excavated and surveyed in five rounds from 2001 to 2005, and designated Historic Site No. 464. Roof tiles inscribed with "惠蔭院" (Hyeeumwon, House of Virtuous Grace) and "惠陰寺" (Hyeeumsa, Temple of Virtuous Grace) were retrieved through the investigations. This paper respected the official report on the investigations regarding the name of the ruins. (*Report on the Excavations of Hyeeumwon Site in Paju, texts concerning the first to fourth rounds* (Yongin: Buried Cultural Properties Research Institute of Dankook University, 2006), p. 36, p. 65)

39) A roof tile excavated from the ruins of Hyeeumwon is inscribed with "庚申年" (year of *gyeongsin*), a zodiac cycle name corresponding to 1140, supporting this assumption.

IV. Royal Kiln Sites of Goryeo

40) Kim Young-Won, "Historical Significance of Gangjin Celadon," a paper presented at a Korea-China-Japan international symposium on the "Past, Present and Future of Gangjin Celadon," jointly sponsored by Gangjin County and Chosun University in 1999.

41) *Report on Excavation of Kangjin-gun Yongun-ri Celadon Kiln Site* (Seoul: National Museum of Korea, 1996-1997). Another report on the excavation and survey of Sadang-ri kiln sites will be published. The Haegang Ceramics Museum published its own report on surface investigations of kiln sites around Gangjin County, under the title *Celadon Kiln Sites in Gangjin*, in 1992.

42) Kim Young-Won, "Study of Goryeo Celadon from Buan Kilns," *Art History Forum No. 22* (Seoul: Korean Fine Art Institute, first half of 2006).

43) *Catalogue 12 Special Exhibition of Ceramics in Koryŏ Dynasty from the Kiln Site of Yu-cheun-ri, Buan-gun, Cholla-Buk-do* (Seoul: Ewha Womans University Museum, 1983).

44) Ken Nomori, "Goryeo Kiln Sites in Buan," *Ceramics 6-6* (Tokyo: Oriental Ceramic Research Institute, 1934); *op.cit.* (Kyoto: Seikansha, 1944).

45) *A Site Survey on the Seashore Region of Puan County, Korea* (Jeonju: Jeonju National Museum, 1999); *Survey Report on Kiln Sites at Yucheon-ri and Jinseo-ri in Buan* (Iksan: Institute of Mahan-Baekjae Cultures of Wonkwang University, 1994); *Report on Excavation and Survey of Celadon Kiln Sites in Zone 7 of Yucheon-ri in Buan* (Iksan: Wonkwang University Museum and Gangjin: Buan County, South Jeolla Province, 2001).

46) *Intermediary Excavation Report on Hyeeumwon Site in Paju* (Yongin: Buried Cultural Properties Research Institute of Dankook University, 2003); Kang Kyung-nam, "Study of Goryeo Celadon from Hyeeumwon Site in Paju -- Chronology and Characteristics," *Study of Cultural History, Volume 21* (Seoul: Korean Society of Cultural History, 2004).

V. Royal Ceramics of Goryeo

47) Choi Sun-u, *op. cit.* (Seoul, 1969).

48) *Report on Excavation and Survey of Hyeeumwon Site in Paju* (Yongin: Buried Cultural Properties Research Institute of Dankook University, 2006), p. 409.

49) A decorative terracotta roof tile with a dragon-headed fish pattern is among artifacts excavated from the royal palace site of Goryeo in Gaesong. An identical object was found from ruins of Hyeeumwon, implying a connection between the two royal sites.

50) KIM Youngmi, *A Vessel for the Soul, Sinan Incense Burners*, compiled by the National Museum of Korea (Seoul: Sahoi Pyoungnon (Social Criticism) Co., 2008), pp. 79-81.

51) Ye Zhemin & Ye Peilan, *Collection of Porcelain Treasures of the Ru Kiln* (Beijing: Beijing Publishing House, 2002).

52) *Ibid.* (Seoul: National Museum of Korea, 1996-1997).

53) *Gangjin Samheung-ri Kiln Site II* (Gwangju: Gwangju National Museum, Damyang: Honam Cultural Property Research Center and Gangjin: the Gangjin/Wando Branch of Korean Rural Corporation, 2004).

54) Jeon Seung-chang, "Study of Celadon Incense Burners with Sculpted Ornaments," *Goryeo Celadon and Religion* (Gangjin: Gangjin Celadon Data Museum, 2002), p. 85.

55) Xu Jing, *op. cit.*, Book 32 "Vessels and Utensils 3"; Xu Jing, *op. cit.*, translated by Jo Dong-won et al. (Seoul: Taurus Books, 2005), p. 388.

56) Jeon Seung-chang, above-cited paper, (Gangjin: Gangjin Celadon Data Museum, 2002), pp. 85-86.

57) Choi Soon-guen, "A Study on the Reconstitution of Rites System in Koryo Dynasty in the 11th and 12th Century," a master's degree thesis, Graduate School of Konkuk University, 1994; Lee Yong-jin, "*Ding*-shaped Celadon Vessels of the Goryeo Period," *Korean Journal of Art History, No. 252* (Seoul: Art History Association of Korea, 2006).

Text and Translation of King Injong's Epitaph

維皇統六年歲在丙寅三月
In the Third Month of the Year of Byeongin (1146), the Sixth Year of Huangtong (reign title of Emperor Gaozong of Southern Song)

王臣明謹再拜稽首上
The King of Goryeo, Hyeon (given name of Uijong), kowtowing with respect and deference,

玉册
presents this Jade Book.

大行大王聰明寬裕博大醇
The Great Preceding King was a brilliant and truthful person with a generous and magnanimous heart.

眞因百姓以爲 心攬萬機而
Taking the people's mind for his own and handling numerous state affairs,

忘食 外郤文華之飾
he forgot eating. Declining gorgeous decoration outwardly,

内無耽樂之從
he never pursued indulgence inwardly.

盛德本之日新 動容中禮
He tried to renew himself everyday by accumulating virtue, and his every deed befitted etiquette.

多能發於天縱 下筆如神
His many talents were endowed by heaven and his writing was divine.

愼刑每極於 哀矜求諫
He was discreet in imposing punishments and always took pity on people. He sought advice.

樂聞其 過失再袷
He enjoyed hearing about his errs. He observed rites for ancestors twice a year.

論經肇 祀圓丘
He discussed state management, and for the first time conducted rites at the Heavenly Altar.

修睦以固約 戡鎬京之亂
He promoted harmony and consolidated treaties, and subdued rebellion in another capital.

則殲魁以靖民 作新宮室
He stabilized the public by defeating the head of the mob, and built a new palace.

之居 興農桑之利
He revived farming and sericulture to benefit people.

王奠邦基於不拔□成則
The King laid a solid and unextractable foundation of the country.

恩濡澤洽 理定功成宜延
The grace reached all corners of the country, and politics were stabilized and meritorious accomplishments attained. Surely,

難老之期以永 丕平之業
he should have lived long, enjoying peace and prosperity.

以曆在而
He should have remained on the throne. However,

焦思所積 邁疾彌留邀彼
with worries accumulated and disease lingering, to his home

帝鄉遽
on the other world, all of a sudden,

逝轉
he departed.

馭閔予眇質虔承
Miserable and pitiable, I will

玉几之 言愴痛玆深攀號
solemnly succeed the words bequeathed. Nevertheless, with the overwhelming grief growing ever deeper,

莫及仰惟
I cry and call out, but it is useless.

號諡式據質文之典或參單
Thinking of your posthumous title based on your disposition and achievements, we also referred to debate on one or two such titles.

複之論夫
Generally,

恭者維德之基
reverence is the basis of virtue,

孝者爲行之本所貴乎道莫
and filial piety is the root of all deeds. As the way to be cherished

尙於
nothing comes ahead of these virtues.

(恭孝)□□□□開府儀同三
The three agencies concerned with rites

司檢校太傅守太尉門下侍
the Crown Prince and

郎同中書門下平(章事)
Chief State Councillor

尊諡曰
presents your posthumous epithet,

恭孝大王廟號(仁宗)
the Great King of Reverence and Filial Piety, and your posthumous title, Injong.

茂實非擬議之 形容追叙
The abundant and plentiful achievements you have bequeathed are beyond debate. Particularly, in memory of your appearance during your lifetime,

殊蹤必奉揚於
your eminent footsteps will be made known broadly.

明靈之如在冀 寶册之是
I beseech your bright soul to accept this treasure book

膺垂 裕無疆流
and grant us unbounded blessing.

仙仗於無何敢薦
To present your posthumous titles this splendid ceremony is conducted.

Translation from Chinese to Korean by Im Jae-wan, consultant for the Suwon Museum

Romanization Key

	Pre-2000 Standard	2000 Revised Standard
Kingdom / Dynasty	Choseon	Joseon
	Chosŏn	Joseon
	Chosun	Joseon
	Koryŏ	Goryeo
	Koryo	Goryeo
	Shilla	Silla
Province	Chŏlla-do	Jeolla Province
	Cholla-Buk-do	North Jeolla Province
	Chŏllabuk-do	North Jeolla Province
	Chŏllanam-do	South Jeolla Province
	Kyŏnggi-do	Gyeonggi Province
	Kyŏngsangbuk-do	North Gyeongsang Province
Island	Daesŏm	Daeseom Island
	Jindo	Jin Island
	Kanghwado	Ganghwa Island
	Wando	Wan Island
City	Kaesŏng	Gaeseong
	Kwangju	Gwangju
	Kyŏngju	Gyeongju
	Jŏnju	Jeonju
	Paju	Paju
	Pohang	Pohang
	Pyŏngyang	Pyongyang
County	Buan-gun	Buan County
	Jangpung-gun	Jangpung County
	Kaepung-gun	Gaepung County
	Kanghwa-gun	Ganghwa County
	Kangjin-gun	Gangjin County
	Pongsŏng-gun	Bongseong County
	Puan County	Buan County
	Puan-gun	Buan County

Decorative Motifs of Goryeo Royal Ceramics

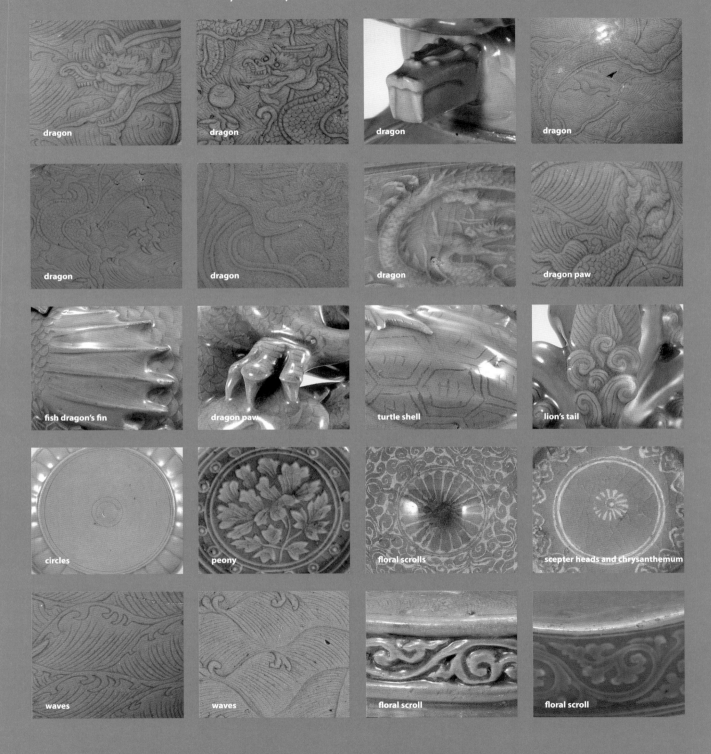

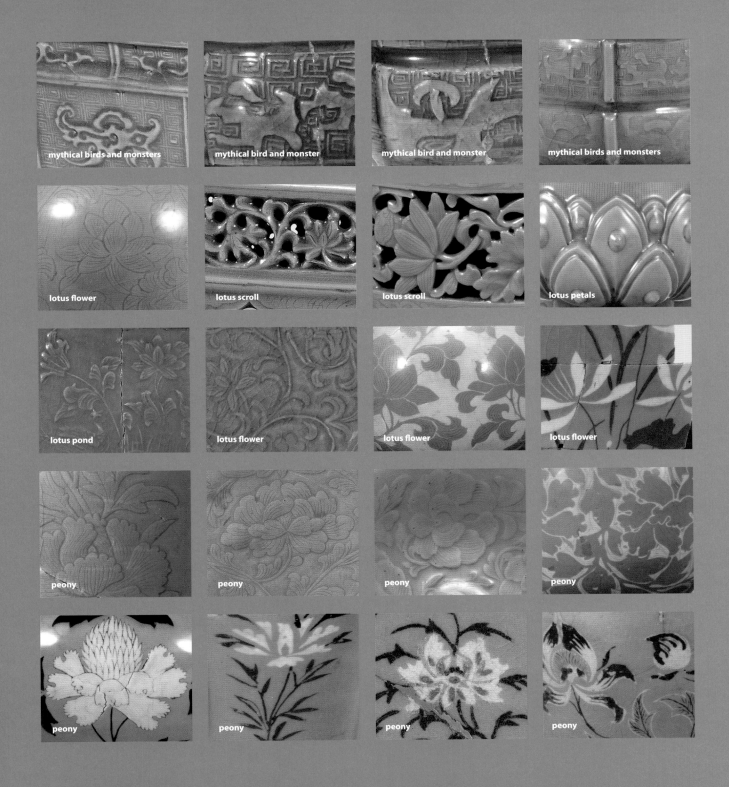

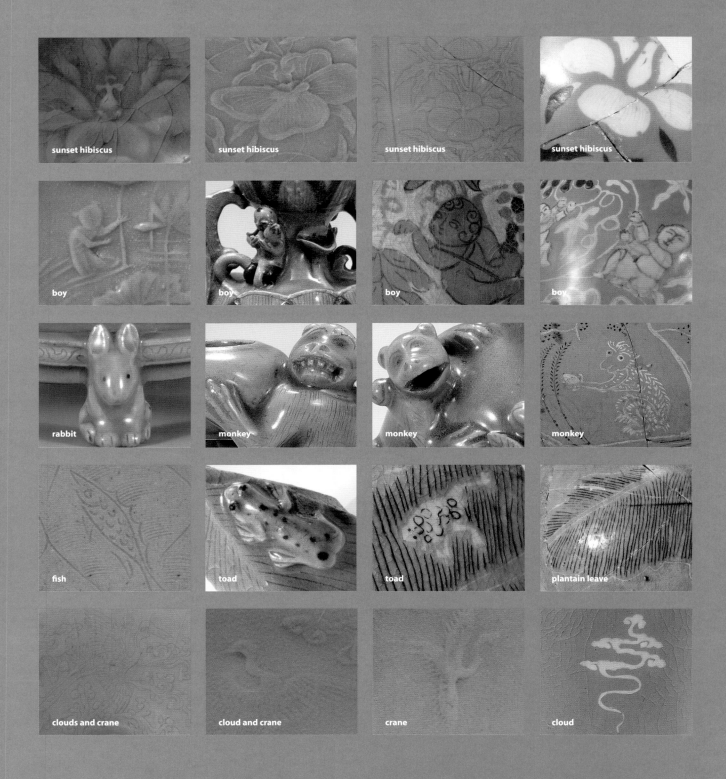

sunset hibiscus

sunset hibiscus

sunset hibiscus

sunset hibiscus

boy

boy

boy

boy

rabbit

monkey

monkey

monkey

fish

toad

toad

plantain leave

clouds and crane

cloud and crane

crane

cloud

List of Plates

Giljeong-ri, Yangdo-myeon, Ganghwa County, Gyeonggi Province
A glass negative of 1923
National Museum of Korea

23. Artifacts excavated from Seongneung, the tomb of King Huijong (r. 1204-1211, died in 1237)
Goryeo, first half of the 13th century
Housed at the National Research Institute of Cultural Heritage

24. Artifacts from Gareung, the tomb of Queen Dowager Sungyeong (?-1236)
Goryeo, first half of the 13th century
Celadon fragment at far left on the back row: Present H. 1.7cm, D. 4.5cm (base)
Housed at the National Research Institute of Cultural Heritage

25. A full view of Golleung, the tomb of Queen Dowager Wondeok (?-1239)
Giljeong-ri, Yangdo-myeon, Ganghwa County, Gyeonggi Province; A glass negative of 1923
National Museum of Korea

26. Artifacts from Golleung, the tomb of Queen Dowager Wondeok (?-1239)
Goryeo, first half of the 13th century
Incense burner at the far right in the back row: H. 8cm, D. 14.7cm (the widest part); Housed at the National Research Institute of Cultural Heritage

27. The old tomb in Neungnae-ri after excavation
Excavated by the National Research Institute of Cultural Heritage in 2006

28. Artifacts from the old tomb in Neungnae-ri
Goryeo, first half of the 13th century
Far right on the front row: Present L. 6.4cm
Left on the back row: H. 9.6cm; Housed at the National Research Institute of Cultural Heritage

III. Goryeo Royal Ceramics from Other Historic Sites

29. A general view of the royal palace site in Gaeseong
A glass negative of 1918
National Museum of Korea

30. Site of Hoegyeongjeon, the main throne hall
A glass negative of 1918
National Museum of Korea

31. Celadon fragments excavated from the royal palace site in Gaeseong
Collected before 1945
Left on the back row: H. 2.3cm
Right on the back row: H. 6.8cm, D. 4cm (rim)

National Museum of Korea

32. Celadon roof tiles
Goryeo, 12th century
Excavated from a kiln site at Sadang-ri
L. 40.8cm (total), W. 20.3cm (concave), D. 8-8.4cm (convex); National Museum of Korea

33. Celadon flattened jar with inlaid monkey and gold ornament
Goryeo, second half of the 13th century
Excavated from the royal palace site in Gaeseong
Present H. 25.5cm, D. 9.3cm (base)
National Museum of Korea

34. Gold-painted design on the side of the flattened jar

35. A general view of the site of Hyeeumwon
Excavated by the Buried Cultural Properties Research Institute of Dankook University in 2001-2004, and the HanBaek Research Institute for Cultural Heritage in 2008

36. A concave roof-end tile inscribed with "Hyeeumwon"
Goryeo, first half of the 12th century to the first half of the 13th century
Excavated from Hyeeumwon site
H. 9.1cm, W. 27.5cm
Excavated by the Buried Cultural Properties Research Institute of Dankook University

37. Roof ridge end tile shaped like a dragon head
Goryeo, first half of the 12th century to the first half of the 13th century
Excavated from Hyeeumwon site; H. 28cm
Excavated by the Buried Cultural Properties Research Institute of Dankook University

38. Celadon lids
Goryeo, 12th century
Excavated from Hyeeumwon site; Right: H. 2.7cm
Excavated by the Buried Cultural Properties Research Institute of Dankook University

39. Celadon bowls
Goryeo, 12th century
Excavated from Hyeeumwon site
Left: H. 6.8cm, D. 19.7cm (rim)
Excavated by the Buried Cultural Properties Research Institute of Dankook University

40. Celadon cups
Goryeo, first half of the 12th century to the first half of the 13th century
Excavated from Hyeeumwon site
Far left: H. 4.3cm, D. 8.6cm (rim), 3.6cm (base)

Far right: H. 7.3cm, D. 8cm (rim), 5cm (base)
Excavated by the Buried Cultural Properties Research Institute of Dankook University

41. Celadon dishes
Goryeo, first half of the 12th century to the first half of the 13th century
Excavated from Hyeeumwon site
Far left: H. 3.4cm, D. 13cm (rim), 6.8cm (base)
Far right: H. 2.3cm, D. 10cm (rim), 8.2cm (base)
Excavated by the Buried Cultural Properties Research Institute of Dankook University

42. Celadon pillow with incised lotus design
Goryeo, 12th century
Excavated from Hyeeumwon site
Present L. 26.6cm, Present W. 10.5cm
Excavated by the Buried Cultural Properties Research Institute of Dankook University

43. Celadon lotus-shaped incense burner
Goryeo, 12th century
Excavated from Hyeeumwon site
Present H. 9.6cm
Excavated by the HanBaek Research Institute for Cultural Heritage

44. Celadon incense burners
Goryeo, first half of the 12th century to the first half of the 13th century
Excavated from Hyeeumwon site
Left: H. 12cm; Right: Present H. 7.4cm
Excavated by the Buried Cultural Properties Research Institute of Dankook University

45. Fragments of celadon plates with inlaid willow and waterfowl
Goryeo, 12th century to the first half of the 13th century; Excavated from Hyeeumwon site
Left: Present L. 10.3cm; Right: Present L. 15.3cm
Excavated by the Buried Cultural Properties Research Institute of Dankook University

46. Celadon shard with a molded toad
Goryeo, 12th century
Excavated from Hyeeumwon site; Present L. 5cm
Excavated by the Buried Cultural Properties Research Institute of Dankook University

47. Fragments of Ding white porcelain and Jingdezhen bluish white porcelain
Song Dynasty of China
Excavated from Hyeeumwon site
Left middle row: H. 7.3cm, D. 10.5cm (rim), 6cm (base); Right: H. 5.2cm, D. 18.2cm (rim), 5.6cm (base); Excavated by the Buried Cultural Properties Research Institute of Dankook University

48. Fragments of celadon, and green-glazed and marble-patterned ceramics
Song Dynasty of China
Excavated from Hyeeumwon site
Front row left: Present H. 2.3cm
Back row right: Present H. 4cm
Excavated by the Buried Cultural Properties Research Institute of Dankook University

IV. Royal Kiln Sites of Goryeo

49. A view of a valley in Daegu-myeon, Gangjin County, where ruins of Goryeo period pottery kilns are clustered
A photo dated 1964; National Museum of Korea

50. Fragment of a celadon plum vase with carved dragon design
Goryeo, 12th century
Excavated from a kiln site at Sadang-ri
Present H. 21cm, Present W. 25.3cm
National Museum of Korea

51. Broken celadon pillow with incised dragon design
Goryeo, 12th century
Excavated from a kiln site at Sadang-ri
H. 10.6cm, L. 21cm (the longest part), W. 15.2cm (the widest part); National Museum of Korea

52. Broken celadon plum vase with carved lotus and sunset hibiscus design
Goryeo, 12th century
Excavated from a kiln site at Sadang-ri
Present H. 31.5cm, D. 14.5cm (base)
National Museum of Korea

53. Celadon shards decorated with peonies
Goryeo, 12th century
Excavated from kiln sites at Sadang-ri
Front row left: H. 5.5cm, D. 3.7cm (base)
Back row right: H. 4.7cm, D. 6.3cm (base)
National Museum of Korea

54. Fragments of celadon chairs with openwork decoration
Goryeo, 12th century
Excavated from kiln sites at Sadang-ri
Back row: Present H. 20.5cm, T. 1.5-2cm
National Museum of Korea

55. Shards of celadon incense burners with carved dragon design
Goryeo, 12th century
Excavated from kiln sites at Sadang-ri
Right: Present H. 11.6cm, Present W. 11.4cm
National Museum of Korea

56. Fragments of celadon with underglaze iron painting or iron glaze
Goryeo, 12th century
Excavated from kiln sites at Sadang-ri
Left: Present L. 11.7cm; Center: Present H. 14.7cm
Right (lid): H. 3.8cm, D. 9.7cm (the widest part)
National Museum of Korea

57. A view of a pottery kiln site at Yucheon-ri, Buan County
A glass negative made before 1945
National Museum of Korea

58. Celadon bowl with inlaid willow, reed and waterfowl
Goryeo, second half of the 12th century to 13th century; Excavated from a kiln site at Yucheon-ri
Donated by Lee Hong-kun
Present H. 5.2cm, D. 4.7cm (base)
National Museum of Korea

59. Celadon incense burner with carved willow, reed and waterfowl
Goryeo, second half of the 12th century to 13th century; Excavated from a kiln site at Yucheon-ri
Donated by Lee Hong-kun
H. 12.7cm, W. 27cm (the widest part)
National Museum of Korea

60. Fragments of a celadon plum vase with inlaid oddly-shaped rocks and waterfowl
Goryeo, second half of the 12th century to 13th century; Excavated from a kiln site at Yucheon-ri
Donated by Lee Hong-kun
Present H. 20.2cm
National Museum of Korea

61. Fragments of a celadon plum vase with inlaid sunset hibiscus
Goryeo, second half of the 12th century to 13th century; Excavated from a kiln site at Yucheon-ri
Donated by Lee Hong-kun
Present H. 24.7cm; National Museum of Korea

62. Celadon pillow with inlaid clouds and cranes
Goryeo, second half of the 12th century to 13th century; Excavated from a kiln site at Yucheon-ri
Donated by Lee Hong-kun
H. 11.1cm, L. 29.4cm (the longest part)
National Museum of Korea

63. Celadon shards with inlaid landscape
Goryeo, second half of the 12th century to 13th century; Excavated from a kiln site at Yucheon-ri
Donated by Lee Hong-kun
Left: Present L. 12.3cm, Present W. 12.8cm
National Museum of Korea

64. Celadon vessel covers
Goryeo, second half of the 12th century to 13th century; Excavated from kiln sites at Yucheon-ri
Donated by Lee Hong-kun
Left: H. 3.9cm; Right: H. 3.8cm, D. 12.5cm
National Museum of Korea

65. Broken celadon cups and stands
Goryeo, second half of the 12th century to 13th century; Excavated from kiln sites at Yucheon-ri
Donated by Lee Hong-kun
Left on the back row: H. 7.4cm, D. 8.2cm (base), 16.2cm (the widest part)
National Museum of Korea

66. Broken celadon dishes with inlaid floral designs
Goryeo, second half of the 12th century to 13th century; Excavated from kiln sites at Yucheon-ri
Donated by Lee Hong-kun
Left on the front row: H. 2.5cm, D. 11.4cm (rim), 7cm (base); Left on the back row: H. 6.4cm
National Museum of Korea

67. Celadon plum vase with inlaid plantain and toads
Goryeo, second half of the 12th century to 13th century; Excavated from a kiln site at Yucheon-ri
Donated by Lee Hong-kun
Present H. 30.8cm; National Museum of Korea

68. Celadon bottle with inlaid lotus and chrysanthemum
Goryeo, second half of the 12th century to 13th century; Excavated from a kiln site at Yucheon-ri
Donated by Lee Hong-kun
H. 34.7cm; National Museum of Korea

69. Porcelain shards
Goryeo, second half of the 12th century to 13th century
Excavated from Kiln Site No. 12 at Yucheon-ri
Right on the back row (incense burner): Present H. 8.5cm, D. 11.5cm (base)
National Museum of Korea

V. Royal Ceramics of Goryeo

70. Celadon ritual ewer carved with willow, reed and waterfowl
Goryeo, 12th century
Excavated in Gaeseong; Treasure No. 344
H. 34.2cm, D. 9.3cm (base)
National Museum of Korea

71. Celadon plum vase with incised lotus scrolls
Goryeo, 12th century; National Treasure No. 97

H. 43.9cm, D. 7.2cm (rim), 15.8cm (base)
National Museum of Korea

72. Fragments of celadon plum vases
Excavated from kiln sites at Sadang-ri
Left: Present H. 8.5cm, D. 6.4cm (rim)
Right: Present H. 17.8cm
National Museum of Korea

73. Celadon plum vase with carved peony scrolls
and dragons
Goryeo, 12th century; Excavated in Gaeseong
H. 37.9 cm, D. 6.1cm (rim), 11.7cm (base)
National Museum of Korea

74. Celadon pomegranate and monkey-shaped
water dropper
Goryeo, 12th century; Excavated in Gaeseong
H. 8cm, D. 7.9cm; National Museum of Korea

75. Celadon turtle-shaped water dropper with
dragon head
Goryeo, 12th century; Excavated in Gaeseong
H. 6.1cm; National Museum of Korea

76. Celadon monkey-shaped ink jar
Goryeo, 12th century
Excavated in Gaeseong; H. 7.1cm
National Museum of Korea

77. Celadon brush stand with dragon heads and
openwork lotus scrolls
Goryeo, 12th century; Excavated in Gaeseong
H. 9cm, L. 17.4cm, W. 4.8cm
National Museum of Korea

78. Celadon turtle-shaped ewer with dragon head
Goryeo, 12th century; Excavated in Gaeseong
National Treasure No. 96; H. 17.3cm
National Museum of Korea

79. Celadon dragon-shaped ewer
Goryeo, 12th century
Excavated in Gaeseong; National Treasure No. 61
H. 24.4cm, D. 10.3cm (base)
National Museum of Korea

80. Celadon foliated dishes
Goryeo, 12th century
Excavated in Gaeseong
H. 3.6cm, D. 17.6cm
National Museum of Korea

81. Celadon foliated cup stand
Goryeo, 12th century; H. 6.7cm
National Museum of Korea

82. Celadon lotus-shaped incense burner
Goryeo, 12th century; Excavated in Gaeseong

H. 15.2cm, D. 10.5cm (rim)
National Museum of Korea

83. Fragment of a celadon lotus-shaped incense
burner
Excavated from a kiln site at Yucheon-ri
Donated by Lee Hong-kun
Present H. 8cm, W. 19.3cm
National Museum of Korea

84. Fragments of celadon lotus-shaped incense
burners
Excavated from kiln sites at Sadang-ri
Right on the back row: Present H. 9.8cm,
W. 15.8cm; National Museum of Korea

85. Celadon incense burner with dragon-shaped
cover
Goryeo, 12th century
Excavated in Gaeseong; H. 22.7cm
National Museum of Korea

86. Celadon incense burner with lion-shaped cover
Goryeo, 12th century
Excavated in Gaeseong
National Treasure No. 60; H. 21.2cm
National Museum of Korea

87. Celadon incense burner with openwork
decoration
Goryeo, 12th century
Excavated in Gaeseong
National Treasure No. 95
H. 15.3cm (total), D. 11.5cm
National Museum of Korea

88. Celadon incense burner with impressed
monsters
Goryeo, 12th century
H. 11.1cm, L. 14.1cm, W. 12.7cm
National Museum of Korea

89. Celadon incense burner with impressed
monsters
Goryeo, 12th century; Excavated in Gaeseong
H. 13.3cm, D. 11.7cm (rim)
National Museum of Korea

90. Fragment of a celadon incense burner with
impressed monsters
Excavated from a kiln site at Sadang-ri
Present H. 13.5cm
National Museum of Korea

91. Celadon bowl carved with lotus pond and
children
Goryeo, 12th century
Excavated in Gaeseong

H. 5.6cm, D. 18.1cm (rim)
National Museum of Korea

92. Celadon pillow with openwork lotus scrolls
Goryeo, 12th century
Excavated in Gaeseong
H. 11.2cm, W. 26.7cm
National Museum of Korea

93. Celadon bowl with inlaid floral scrolls
Goryeo, circa 1159
Excavated from the tomb of Mun Gong-yu
(?-1159) in Gaepung County, Gyeonggi Province
National Treasure No. 115
H. 6.2cm, D. 16.8cm (rim), 4.4cm (base)
National Museum of Korea

94. Celadon plum vase with inlaid bamboo and
cranes
Goryeo, second half of the 12th century to 13th
century; Treasure No. 903; H. 38.9cm, D. 5.1cm (rim)
Private collection

95. Fragments of celadon plum vases with inlaid
willow design
Excavated from kiln sites at Yucheon-ri
Donated by Lee Hong-kun
Left : Present H. 10.3cm
National Museum of Korea

96. Celadon gourd-shaped ewer with inlaid peony
scrolls
Goryeo, second half of the 12th century to 13th
century; National Treasure No. 116
H. 34.3cm, D. 2cm (rim), 9.7cm (base)
National Museum of Korea

97. Celadon plum vase with inlaid peony and
underglaze copper-red decoration
Goryeo, second half of the 12th century to
13th century
Excavated in Gaeseong
Treasure No. 346
H. 34.5cm, D. 5.8cm (rim), 13.2cm (base)
National Museum of Korea

Index